Crazy Quilted
Heirlooms & Gifts

J. Marsha Michler

Published by

Krause Publications
700 East State Street
Iola, WI 54990-001
www.krause.com

Please call or write for our free catalog of publications. Our toll-free number to place an order or obtain a free catalog is 800-258-0929 or please use our regular business telephone 715-445-2214.

Library of Congress Catalog Number 2001088584
ISBN 0-87341-959-6

Some products in this book are registered trademakrs of their respective copanies: Pearl Crown Rayon , Basting & Bobbin, YLI Select and YLI 100% Cotton Quilting Thread, 1000, all registered by YLI.
Silk Serica is a registered trademark of Kreinik Mfg. Co. Inc.

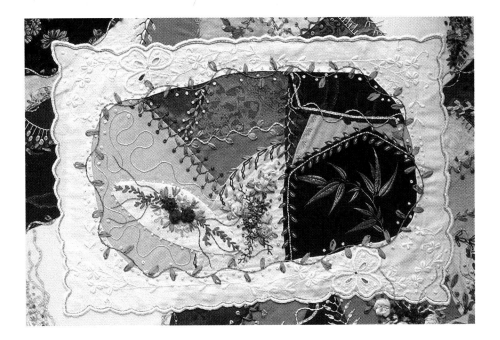

Dedication

This book is dedicated to the memory of my grandmother, E.K.M., who was a gardener, needleworker, homeworker, craftswoman, wife, mother, grandmother, and so much more, and from whom I learned that strong women are indeed the mighty oaks of civilization.

Acknowledgments

Each book that I have done has been a treasure to me. This one, like those before, is a composite both of ideas nurtured into tangible forms, and of all the people associated with my life at the time I wrote it, both professionally and personally. A very great many thanks to all of them including my excellent agent, Sandy Taylor, the wonderful and professional folks at Krause Publications who are a joy to work with, but most especially: my hard-working editors Amy Tincher-Durik and Christine Townsend, and book designer, Marilyn Hochstatter. On a personal level I am immensely grateful to Carolyn and Dave for the many fireside chats, for hosting the photography sessions, and for shelter from the storm (indubitably!). I would be remiss not to mention Bear-Bear, a cooperative model and happy companion, who also sets a wonderful example as herder and caretaker of eleven cats. And always and ever, many thanks to my son, Ben, for being so understanding through all that life brings. Thanks to all of my family for being there. Thanks, too, to Dena Lenham of Kreinik Co. Inc., Vicki Smith of YLI Corporation, and Maggie Backman of Things Japanese for keeping me supplied.

Table of Contents

Introduction

Two methods of Crazy Quilting

The Projects

Introduction

We are enjoying a revival of crazy quilting, a form of creative quilting with its roots in the Victorian age. Although crazy quilting lapsed into near-obscurity over most of the 1900's, it has now returned to popularity with signs of becoming a permanent presence in the fields of quilting and the needlearts. And no wonder: the irresistible appeal of this textile art form is a combination of its adaptability to many forms and the many materials including fabrics, threads, laces, and trims that can be incorporated. From plain to fancy, anything goes.

I felt compelled to assemble a volume of projects after doing two books about crazy quilts: *The Magic of Crazy Quilting*, and *Crazy Quilts by Machine*. Although I still believe there is nothing more satisfying than finishing a crazy quilt, I very much enjoyed dreaming up this collection of mostly smaller things. This book presents a limited selection of the many possible ideas to which crazy quilting can be applied.

There are no "skill levels" given with the projects. Most of the projects can be done by anyone who has basic sewing and/or needlearts skills. If you are a beginner with little sewing experience, you may want to first try a project with relatively simple finishing details such as a pillow or placemats and then, as you gain proficiency, attempt those that are more detailed. A read through any of the project instructions should give you an idea if the project is one that you wish to attempt or not.

Crazy quilting is...

A form of quilting in which odd-shaped pieces of fabrics are assembled into a whole. In one version, which I call the Antique Method, patches of mostly fancy fabrics are placed onto a foundation layer of fabric then fastened in place by embroidery. In another that I call Confetti Piecing, cotton quilting fabrics are sewn together and the finished piece can be tied or quilted.

How This Book Came About

One day I stayed home. That was the day I suddenly decided to no longer accrue wages from an employer who did not allow my creativity to freely range the plains of possibility. Enough, I said. This is my life and my time and I want to spend it otherwise.

And staying home was a wondrous delight. Out came the scraps and the scissors and with no further ado this book was born. Newly scribbled sketches of projects-to-be were tacked upon my walls and my once nearly abandoned studio jumped into life. Sorted piles of scraps and trims turned the floor into a hilly terrain of ideas. The cat loved it. What fun she had jumping into the piles and later curling up among them. The dog, on the other hand, peered into the doorway, then sidled away, glancing back over his shoulder—what had happened to his refuge? His place on the futon was now heaped with fabrics in wondrous hues.

The sewing machine whirred and the iron spluttered. Occasionally people stopped by the doorway and looked in. Who were they—family, friends? I hardly noticed. I was far into my journey and nothing could stop me until I finished.

Soon the projects escaped the studio, and the living room took on a new look. The dining room was soon to follow. A new tea set brightened the kitchen. The family's tiniest tot was newly outfitted. My Mister went to work in a new tie and came home to a new bathrobe, and even the dog now proudly strutted under his prized new jacket.

So here it is. I hope you enjoy this book and I hope you make many wonderful things for your friends, family, and yourself (you should always be on your own gift list). And now let's accept that some of the above is rumor while scraps of it may be hovering near the truth. Sincerely, enjoy!

Both of the patching methods, the Antique Method and Confetti Piecing, are suitable for beginners to those who are experienced. Each method employs a very different approach. If you have done traditional quilting or garment sewing, you may be comfortable trying a Confetti "crazy" project using familiar quilting cottons. If you have done hand needlework, the Antique Method may be the most comfortable for you.

Any of the projects can be made using either of the two methods. An explanation for how to substitute one method for the other is given on page 17. I suggest learning both methods, and using the one that seems more appropriate for the project at hand. Do you want the project to be quilted?—use Confetti Piecing. Would you rather have it hand embroidered?—use the Antique Method.

Any of the projects in this book can become heirlooms. Sometimes heirlooms are thought of as frilly or delicate things that are used once, then stored away for a generation or two. Not so the ones in this book! I'd like to propose a different way of defining an heirloom: an item of superior (that is, quality) construction, while also being useful and used. Giving the next

generation a much used and loved object that was made carefully by hand is a way of handing down craftsmanship. So it faded a bit—it was loved!

How to Use This Book

First, learn one or both of the crazy quilting methods unless you already have a preferred method. After choosing a project, read through the instructions thoroughly before beginning. Also, check with Basic Techniques in the back of the book for those that are relevant to your project. Then, assemble the materials and begin.

 the Confetti Method of crazy quilting, or a machine method

the Antique Method of crazy quilting, or a by-hand method

Guidelines for Washing Silk, Wool, and Other Fine Fabrics

All fine, washable fabrics can be treated to this gentle bath. Some dry-clean-only fabrics may also be washed gently. Fabrics that are labeled "dry clean only" could continually bleed dye, in which case the fabric should not be considered washable. In some fabrics, such as acetate moiré, and bengaline, some surface finish may be lost. Test-wash a small piece to see if there are any changes.

Use lukewarm water with a mild soap dissolved in it. Unscented natural shampoo is my first choice for a mild soap—find this at a natural foods store.

Soak the fabrics without agitation for several minutes. If washing wool, use absolutely no agitation. Wool begins to felt if it is agitated in water, and it shrinks if subjected to temperature extremes whether in washing or in drying. Silks and other fine fabrics may be lightly agitated. Drain the water, refill with lukewarm water and soak or lightly agitate the fabrics again, and drain. Repeat the process until all traces of soap are removed. Roll the fabric in a bath towel to soak up excess water, then line dry.

Two Methods of Crazy Quilting

Materials and Tools for the Antique Method of Crazy Patching

- Fabric for foundation: 100-percent unbleached muslin, batiste or silk organza (see the individual projects for recommended foundations) in white or off-white
- Patch fabrics as called for in instructions for individual projects
- Basting thread* and hand-sewing needle such as a size 12 sharp
- Embroidery threads (see page 10)
- Embroidery needles in assorted sizes
- Embellishments as desired (see individual projects)

*YLI Basting & Bobbin thread is the type I used. One spool of 800 yards was sufficient for all the projects in this book. This thread does not require waxing to prevent tangles. It is perfect for basting, but is not strong enough for hand or machine sewing of seams.

Tools required are shears for cutting fabric, an iron and ironing board, and pins. For large projects, use an ironing board that is placed up to a table or desk. This is to support the project while providing sufficient working space. For all projects, lower the board so you can sit comfortably in a chair while patching.

The Antique Method of Crazy Patching

This is the method that was most often used by the first makers of crazy quilts, the Victorian needleworkers. It is my favorite method of patching because it is easy, relaxing and creative. Patches are first laid onto a foundation layer of fabric and fitted together by over- and underlapping them. Patches can be moved about to find the best placement, and laces and other trims can be added into the seams before all is basted together. Later, embroidery is used to secure the patches.

How large to make the individual patches is a personal choice. In some projects the patches should be made large enough to accommodate embellishments. In others, the patches are made a size that will be in scale with the project. Observe the photos of the projects to see the approximate number of patches that were used.

For the foundation layer, muslin made of 100-percent cotton is a choice fabric for beginners. It has the firmness needed for many of the projects in this book, and for quilts and wallhangings.

I use quality unbleached muslin. Some of the projects require a lighter weight foundation, such as 100-percent batiste, or silk organza. See the individual projects for the recommended foundation fabric.

Always prewash the foundation fabric. Wash cottons in hot water and line or machine dry. Use the hand-washing guidelines given on page 7 to wash silk organza.

As you add patches to the foundation, lift the foundation occasionally and check that it remains smooth. Eliminate any bunching that occurs by re-pinning or re-basting, and lightly pressing if needed. Bunching will cause the size of the piece to be smaller than it should be, and pieces of the project may not fit together properly.

When choosing fabrics, note the types and colors as called for by the individual projects. Collect 100-percent cottons such as sateen, lightweight twill, velveteen, damask, chintz, and others. Also find 100-percent acetates such as satin, moiré, and taffeta. Other excellent patch fabrics include rayons, lightweight wools, and silks. Silks are welcome in almost any crazy patch project. The heavier ones include noil, dupionni, and broadcloth. Medium-weight silks are the 8 mm and heavier habotai, jacquards, and others. Many of these fabric types are available where garment and drapery fabrics are sold.

1. Beginning in a corner, lay the first patch and pin. Cut this piece rounded or with a wide angle. Optional: you can press under the edges of the patch (those that are not the raw edges of the foundation) as you lay the patch, or lay several patches and go back and press edges under later as in step 3 below.

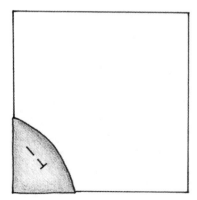

2. Cut out another patch, and lay it so that it underlaps the first by at least 1/2", and pin. This and each consecutive patch is cut to fit into spaces left by former patches. Continue to add and pin patches, having them over- and underlap 1/2" or more.

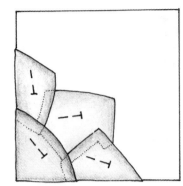

3. After laying patches on a section of the foundation, go back and press under the overlapping edges 1/4". When finished there should be no raw edges showing except at the sides of the foundation. If any gaps occur, add a small patch to fill in the area, or cover the gap with a piece of wide ribbon. Continue laying patches and pressing until the foundation is covered.

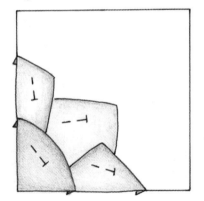

4. If laces are to be added into the seams, place them and pin, concealing all raw edges under patches. Also place any addi-

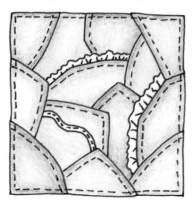

Embroidery Threads

Embroidery threads for working the rows of embroidery along patch seams include:

> *Size 8 pearl cotton*
> *Pearl Crown Rayon*

> *Twisted silks such as:*
> *Soie Perlee*
> *Soie Gobelin (lighter than Perlee)*
> *Silk Serica*
> *Kanagawa or YLI 1000 denier silk embroidery thread*

Pearl cottons come in various thicknesses, and it is the size 8 that is most often used for crazy quilt embroidery. Pearl Crown Rayon is 100-percent rayon, giving it greater sheen than the others. The different types of silks vary in thickness, and all have the characteristic luster of this luxurious fiber.

All of these are twisted threads, not flosses, that have a luster or sheen. The twist gives them texture that allows them to show up well on most fabrics. Any of the threads can be used on any type of fabrics, and mixed or matched on any project. For an all-silk project, however, silk threads are preferable.

Collect and try a variety of twisted embroidery threads. Some are sure to become your favorites.

Note: Some of the stitch diagrams are shown reversed, in boxes, to be used by left-handed sewers.

tional trims (gimpes, braids, ribbons, etc.) that must have their ends concealed under patches. Baste these in place (see step 5), then use regular sewing thread or embroidery stitches to secure them.

5. Place the patched foundation on a flat surface (use a desk or table protected by a cutting mat) and hand-baste all pressed-under edges of patches. The basting stitches should be about 1/2" to 3/4" in length. End by basting around the entire piece. The piece is now ready to be embroidered and embellished. After the patches are secured by embroidery, remove the basting stitches.

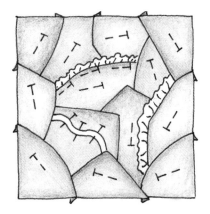

Embroidery Stitches

Embroidery stitches are what hold the patches in place for the Antique Method. Keep this in mind as you embroider, placing the stitches to adequately secure the edges. If you can reach a finger under a patch after it is embroidered, there is too much gap. Often one row of stitches works well, but sometimes a second row is needed.

Some of the stitches make an ideal first row. These include the Feather, Cretan, Blanket, and the Herringbone stitch. Others can be added to these including the Star, the French Knot, the Lazy Daisy, the Fly, and the Straight Stitch. Observe the photos throughout the book to see how stitch combinations and thread colors are used.

Some of the basic embroidery stitches are diagrammed below. If you are a beginner to embroidery, learn the stitches by trying them on scrap fabric. It is good to try to keep the sizes of them consistent, but don't get too fussy about making them perfectly even. Stitches with some unevenness will add character to your work.

Backstitch

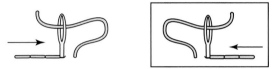

The Backstitch is ideal for narrow outlines (the reverse of the stitch resembles the Outline Stitch).

Bring the needle up a stitch length ahead of the row of stitching and back down in the same hole where the last stitch ended.

Blanket Stitch

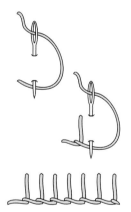

The Blanket Stitch is excellent for fastening down the edges of crazy patches, and can be worked in either a straight or meandering line. Working the stitches very closely forms the Buttonhole Stitch.

Stitch with the needle facing downward, working toward the right or the left (this stitch can be made in either direction).

Detached Buttonhole Stitch

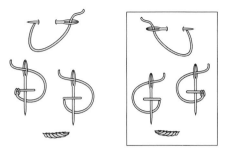

The Detached Buttonhole is a dimensional stitch that can be used for delicate leaves, and for embellishing a row of stitches placed along a crazy patch seam.

First, a plain horizontal stitch is made. Bring the needle up near one end, and work the same as the Blanket Stitch, working over the horizontal stitch and not through the fabric and making the individual stitches close together.

Bullion Stitch

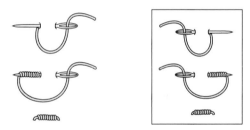

Often used in Wool Embroidery (see page 98), the Bullion Stitch is easiest to learn using wool, but can also be made of silk, cotton, rayon, or other threads. It is a dimensional stitch that can be used for flower petals or leaves in floral embroideries.

Beginning next to where the thread came through the fabric, make a stitch the length the finished stitch is to be, and do not pull through. Wrap the tip of the needle evenly with enough wraps to equal the length of the stitch just made. Hold the wraps between your thumb and forefinger while pulling the needle through. Tug a little to settle the wraps in place. Make a stitch through to the back in the same hole where the stitch first began.

Chain Stitch

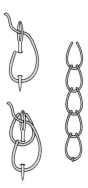

Use single or multiple rows of Chain Stitch to hold crazy patch edges in place, making the rows straight or meandering.

This stitch is made the same as the Lazy Daisy Stitch except instead of tacking the loop with a small stitch, begin the next stitch inside the loop of the first. Continue.

Couching

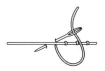

Couching fastens a fiber or thread to the surface of fabric using a second thread to make small tacking stitches. Metal threads, chenille, narrow ribbons, and yarns can be couched.

First, fasten on the thread or fiber that is to be couched. If it is a heavy fiber, bring the ends to the back using a large needle such as a size 18 Chenille needle. Then fasten on a second thread and use it to make tiny stitches over the first one.

Cretan Stitch

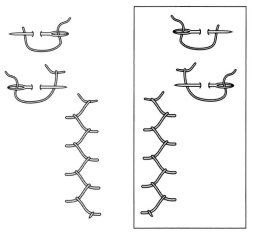

The Cretan Stitch can be straight or meandering, and is attractive when decorated with French Knots or other singular stitches.

Make this stitch the same as the Feather Stitch but make the side stitches horizontally as shown in the diagram.

Feather Stitch

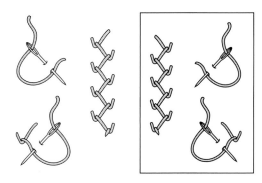

Commonly found in many antique crazy quilts, this stitch is a favorite for holding patch edges in place.

Working downwards, take a stitch first to the right and then the left of an imaginary line. Form the side stitches at a slant as shown in the diagram.

Double Feather Stitch

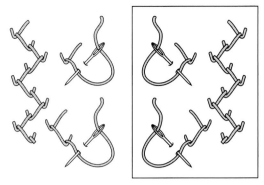

This is a fancier version of the Feather Stitch, but is just as easy to make.

Work this stitch the same as the Feather Stitch, but with an extra stitch made to each side.

Fern Stitch

The Fern Stitch is excellent for working along the edges of crazy patches, and also as foliage in floral embroideries.

First make a vertical Straight Stitch, followed by a series of Fly Stitches working downwards.

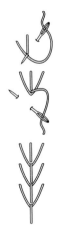

Fly Stitch

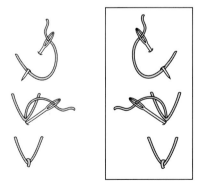

This versatile stitch has many uses. Make them in rows or scatter them across a patch, or nestle a flower in the top of one.

Follow the diagram, making a slanting stitch with the thread running under the needle. Finish with a short stitch, holding the "v" in place.

French Knot

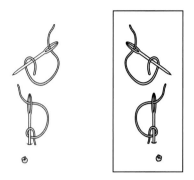

Add these little dimensional dots to rows of other stitches, or use them to form flower centers. An excellent stitch to make in silk ribbon, but for this purpose keep the wraps loose.

Wrap the thread around the needle once, twice, or three or more times in the direction shown. Pierce the fabric next to where the thread came through, pull the wraps snug, and pull through. The more wraps, the larger the stitch.

Pistil Stitch

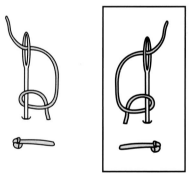

A French Knot with a "tail," the Pistil Stitch is useful in floral embroidery. Also make it in groups to form small fans, and add these to rows of embroidery along patch seams.

Make the stitch the same as the French Knot, but bring the needle through further away.

Herringbone Stitch

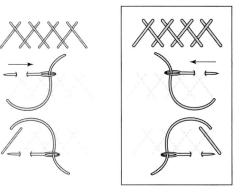

The Herringbone Stitch is ideal for fastening the edges of crazy patches.

Working towards the right, make one stitch at the upper, and the next at the lower of two parallel imaginary lines. The needle faces towards the left.

Closed Herringbone Stitch

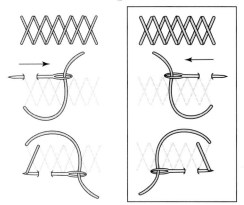

For the Closed Herringbone, make the stitches so close together that the holes made by the previous stitch are shared by the next. This creates an unbroken line of stitches on the reverse side of the work.

Lazy Daisy Stitch

Use Lazy Daisy stitches to decorate rows of stitching along crazy patch edges, and also as flower petals in floral embroideries.

Beginning next to where the thread came through the fabric, make a stitch looping the thread under the tip of the needle as shown. Pull through, then make a tiny stitch over the loop to hold it in place.

Outline Stitch/Reversed Backstitch

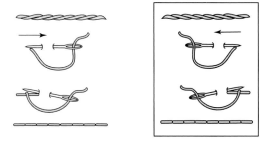

This stitch can be made so the reverse of the work resembles the Backstitch, or the individual stitches can be slightly overlapped, thus creating a wider Outline Stitch. Use it in straight or meandering lines to fasten the edges of crazy patches, or to outline the edges of embroidery motifs (see Embroidering an Initial, page 128).

With the needle facing previous stitches, make a small stitch ending where the last one began.

Running Stitch

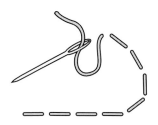

This is the stitch for fastening the layers of a quilt together: make tiny stitches with quilting thread. Using embroidery threads, work the Running Stitch in straight or meandering lines along the edges of crazy patches.

Make a series of stitches in a line.

Satin Stitch

Used to fill in outlined areas, the Satin Stitch is worked closely in one or two layers to completely cover the background fabric. Use it to fill in outlined embroidery motifs using cotton, rayon, or silk floss.

Bring the needle up one side, and down on the other, and repeat. The back of the fabric will be covered the same as the front. Work over an area a second time to fill in more thickly.

Star Stitch

The Star Stitch is excellent for embellishing a row of stitching such as Feather or Cretan Stitches.

Make two stitches crossing each other, then two more crossing in different directions. An extra stitch can be made at the center to hold the crossings in place.

Straight Stitch

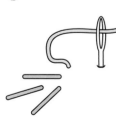

Possibly the simplest of stitches, but several can be grouped to form fanciful flowers or fans.

This is simply one stitch made anywhere, of any size, repeated or not.

The Confetti Method of Crazy Piecing

Confetti Piecing is a machine method, which mainly uses the cotton quilting fabrics used in traditional quilting. It is a quick method that requires neither foundation, embroidery, nor embellishment. The resulting piecing appears complex, as if someone spent hours fitting shapes together. The reality, however, is that very little thought is needed. One quick "cut 'n sew" follows another until the piece is as jumbled as you want it to be. The more cut-and-sews done, the smaller the individual pieces will become. Keep in mind, however, that the smaller the pieces, the more seams there will be to contend with.

Confetti pieced projects can be machine embroidered, machine quilted or tied. It is not readily adaptable to hand embroidery, but if you wish to do so, first baste a piece of foundation fabric onto the back of the work. This prevents disturbing the many seams.

There is no short way to describe this method, although it is much easier to do than the many words and instructions would make it appear. Basically, you cut the pieced fabric in two, then take one of the pieces and sew it back on somewhere else, and repeat. Continue until the piecing is the way you like it: either with very small pieces, or larger ones. See the individual project photos for suggestions.

1. Begin by stacking the eight fabrics evenly. On the cutting mat, cut a 4-3/4" section from one end. Use the 4-3/4" x 9" cut as follows. Note: when using 1/3 yard

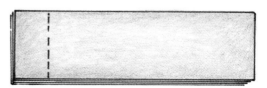

Materials and Tools for Confetti Piecing

- 1/4 yard lengths of 100-percent cotton fabrics for quilting (see individual projects for colors), 8 coordinating prints. Some solids may be used in place of some of the prints, and other medium-weight 100-percent cotton fabrics such as flannel, lightweight twill, or broadcloth may be substituted for some of the quilting cottons.
- 100-percent cotton sewing thread to blend with the fabrics
- Iron and ironing board, rotary cutter, acrylic ruler, 24" x 36" cutting mat, pins

Prewash the fabrics by hand or machine. Line or tumble dry, and press.

Use a 1/4" seam allowance, and press seams to one side. For accuracy, and so the piece lies flatter, steam pressing is desirable as the piece accumulates seams. I prefer to use a dry iron and a spray bottle of water rather than a steam iron. All pressing is done on the right side by folding the new seam away from yourself and pressing into the roll of the fabric.

You will need to move from the sewing machine to the ironing board, and from ironing board to the cutting mat, so it is best to have these areas all within easy reach of each other.

lengths of fabric, make the cut 6-1/4" x 12".

2. Place any two of the fabrics right sides together and machine sew along one long edge to make a square block. Repeat for two more of the fabrics. Press the seams.

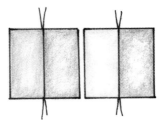

3. Place the remaining fabrics, right sides together, one at each end of the blocks just sewn, and sew them on to make two rectangular blocks. Press the seams.

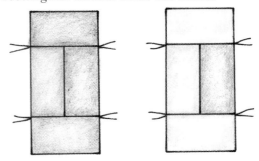

4. Place one of the blocks on the cutting mat and use the ruler and rotary cutter to make a diagonal cut anywhere on the block.

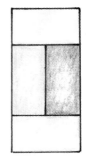

4 a. Take one of the halves and place it right sides together with the remaining block, and cut the block along the cut edge of the diagonal piece. Remove the cut-off piece and sew a seam along the two aligned edges. You may want to first pin the edges, especially if the seam is a long one, before sewing. Place the two remaining pieces together and sew along the diagonal edge. Press.

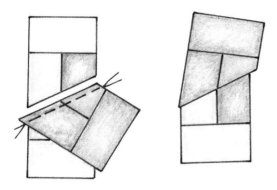

5. Repeat step 4. Make the cuts where you choose. At some point unite the two blocks into one. Continue to cut and sew to make the block the size required for the project.

Substituting the Methods

For any of the projects, Confetti Piecing may be substituted for the Antique Method, and vice versa. Exceptions to this may include the all-silk projects such as the Silk Tie and the Silk Evening Scarf for which the Antique Method is preferable because silk fabrics are easier to handle if laid by hand onto a foundation.

To use the Antique Method for a project written for Confetti Piecing, cut the muslin foundation fabric to the size or shape indicated for the Confetti project. Patch, embellish, and embroider according to instructions for the Antique Method.

To use Confetti Piecing for a project written for the Antique Method, follow instructions for Confetti Piecing, making a piece the size or shape that is required for the foundation. A foundation of muslin or a batting may be added depending on the amount of thickness desired.

Complete the project according to instructions for assembly. Eliminate any quilting or machine couching for those projects done in the Antique Method and use hand embroidery instead. For those worked in Confetti Piecing, observe the different ways the Confetti projects throughout the book are quilted, and use that which best fits the project you are making.

Chapter 1

For the Parlour

Crazy quilted pieces add warmth and elegance to the decor of a room.

Featured Needleart:

Cross-stitch Embroidery Using Waste Canvas

This luxurious living room set is built around a peachy-shades color scheme and a Victorian motif. Dear to the hearts of the Victorians were creatures of the insect world. Bugs and butterflies were oft portrayed needleart subjects, and the simple bug worked here in cross-stitch is an example. The Victorians were also fascinated by plants that grow in water, such as the cattails in the vintage needlepoint on the pillow, and the water lilies in the oil-painted velvet center of the quilt.

Projects:

Fringed Throw

Fringed Pillow with Needlepoint Center

Drapery Tiebacks

Showpiece Wall Quilt

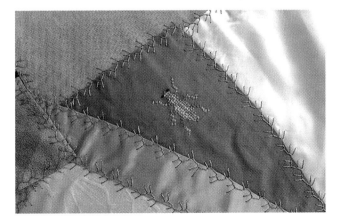

A vintage needlepoint provides a focal point for a crazy quilted pillow.

The antique textiles such as the needlepoint used for the pillow, and the painting on velvet used for the quilt center are "finds" that I came across while browsing through antiques shops. You are not likely to find the same pieces I have found, or even similar ones. Needlepoint pieces portraying floral designs are the most common—many were originally made for chair seats and footstool covers. Other types of needlework may also be substituted. For a quilt center, look for cross-stitch, needlepoint, or a piece of crewel embroidery. For the pillow center, any sturdy piece of needlework can be used, such as needlepoint, crewelwork, or a knitted or crocheted design worked in wool or sturdy cotton.

You may wish to adapt the colors of fabrics, embroidery thread, and fringe to

Pieces such as this painting on velvet can be found while rummaging through antique shops.

Graceful ferns may suggest an idea for doing an embroidery, painting, or other embellishment on fabric.

pick up on the colors in your found pieces. Choose a main color, and then add compatible shades and several neutrals. The Fringed Throw shown is worked in light shades of peach and neutral colors, while the remaining projects make use of stronger, contrasting tones.

Choose fabrics that have luxurious finishes or interesting surface textures. Those used here include drapery moiré, a coarsely woven lightweight wool, plush cotton velveteen, acetate satin, and others. Finishes such as these bring both elegance and diversity to a crazy patched project. These fabric types can often be found where garment and drapery types are sold. If you are purchasing drapery fabrics, choose those that are unbacked, and not too heavy to be workable.

One of the most popular forms of needlework, cross-stitch embroidery, makes a delightful addition to a crazy quilt. With the use of waste canvas in place of even-weave fabric, designs can be worked onto any plain piece of fabric. The waste canvas is basted to the fabric and the design is worked. Finally, the waste canvas is removed by pulling out and discarding the individual threads.

Although cross-stitch designs are commonly available in leaflet, magazine, and book form, you may also try designing your own. Use a finely-gridded graph paper (about fourteen squares to the inch), or use a computer program for cross-stitch design. Also consider using parts of a larger design, isolating parts of it to use as motifs. Some of the motifs on the Showpiece Wall Quilt are "borrowed" from my larger sampler designs.

Embroidery materials for working cross-stitch on crazy patches.

Cross-stitch Embroidery Using Waste Canvas

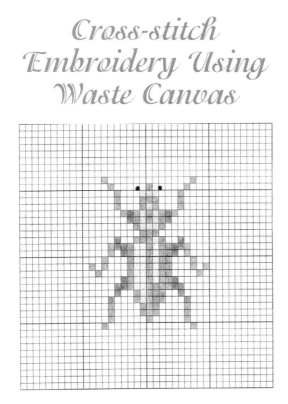

1. To embroider the bugs, baste one 3" square of waste canvas onto each patch to be embroidered.

2. The tapestry needle has a blunt point that will pass between the fibers of the waste canvas. Do not sew through these fibers or they will be difficult to remove later. Cut a working length of the floss, and remove two strands. Hold these together as one, and thread the needle. On the back of the piece, take two or more tiny stitches into the foundation to secure the end, then bring the needle up through to make the first stitch. Work the colors according to the chart beginning at the top of the bug's head, and finishing all of the stitches of one color before beginning another.

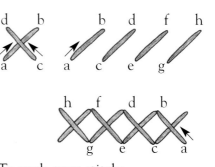

3. To work cross-stitch:
a. Cross all stitches in the same direction. To work a single stitch, begin at the lower left and stitch to the upper right. Then bring the needle through at the lower right and stitch to the upper left.
b. To work a row in one color, work the first part of the stitch across, turn and work the second part going back to the start of the row.

4. When the cross-stitch design is completed, remove the waste canvas. Begin at the edges and pull the warp and weft fibers out of the weave. Those that have cross-stitches worked over them must be pulled carefully in order to not disturb the stitches. Pull them out one at a time until all are removed.

5. Sew a seed bead to each side of the bug's head using the bead thread and a fine needle.

Materials

A small graphed design such as the bug shown here
Waste canvas, one 3" square for each bug to be embroidered (Waste canvas can often be found where needlepoint canvas is sold.)
6-strand cotton embroidery floss, one skein each of 4 shades: pale, medium, and dark rust, and medium taupe
Size 26 tapestry needle
Needle and thread for basting
Seed beads in brown or black, 2 beads for each bug embroidered, fine needle, and black beading thread

ᖴringed Throw

Finished size: 43" square not including the fringe.

The Fringed Throw in a hearthside setting.

Materials

44" square of 100-percent cotton muslin for foundation
1/4 yard lengths of 8 or more fabrics for patches such as cotton velveteen, light-weight wool, drapery moiré, bengaline, acetate satin, and cotton sateen in pastel and light shades of peach, sage, taupe, camel, rose, gray, off-white, including a soft plaid. Save any leftover scraps to use in the remaining projects in this chapter.
YLI Basting & Bobbin thread
2 spools of Pearl Crown Rayon thread, gold.
Waste canvas, 6-strand embroidery floss, beads for bug embroideries (see Cross-stitch Embroidery using waste canvas on page 22)
5 yards of 4" bullion fringe, peach, or any coordinating color
Sewing thread to match the bullion fringe
44" square of plain cotton fabric for backing
Size 8 pearl cotton thread, peach, or any blending color

1/2" seam allowance is used for assembly.

Choose your fabrics carefully to have a mix of textures for this elegant throw. Wool and velveteen fabrics are warm and inviting, while satins and moiré speak of luxury. A graceful bullion fringe accentuates the soft drape of the throw. If you wish to make a throw that is hand-washable, choose washable fabrics and prewash them.

The throw is kept simple. No laces or other trims are added. Embroidery along patch seams is worked in gold Pearl Crown Rayon thread using only one stitch, the Double Feather Stitch. Cross-stitched, Victorian-style bugs scattered about the quilt top, are the sole embellishment. The beauty of elegant fabrics shines through, with a drapey fringe the only frill. You may want to keep this for yourself; however, it would also make a grand wedding gift made in the favorite decorating color of the bride and groom.

1. Patch the 44" square muslin foundation following the Antique Method on page 8. Make most of the patches about 6" to 8" across. Baste the patches, and baste around the quilt.

2. Embroider along patches using Pearl Crown Rayon thread and Double Feather Stitch. Place the stitches so they secure the patches well.

3. Embroider cross-stitch bugs on some of the patches, following instructions for Cross-stitch Embroidery on page 22. Nine bugs were worked randomly onto the throw shown.

4. Pin the fringe onto the right side of the throw having the header of the fringe even with the raw edge of the throw. Begin and end at a corner, or at the center of one side. Snip through the fringe header at each corner in order to turn the corner. Butt the ends of the fringe together to avoid a gap. Baste and press.

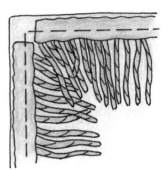

5. With right sides together, pin the backing to the throw and the fringe header and sew around, leaving an opening to turn. Turn right side out. Press. Slipstitch the opening closed.

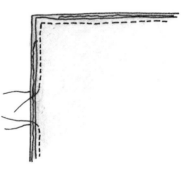

Use pearl cotton thread to tie the quilt, (see page 142) making the stitches just under the edges of patches so they won't show. Make the ties on the back.

Fringed Pillow with Needlepoint Center

Finished size of pillow: 18" square not including the fringe.

The Needlepoint Center Pillow is a colorful accent piece.

Materials

A piece of needlepoint* (the one used here is 9-1/2" x 11")

19" square of 100-percent cotton muslin for foundation

Fabrics for patches: same as those used for the Fringed Throw, plus black and burgundy (or choose colors to go with the piece of needlepoint that you will be using).

YLI Basting & Bobbin thread

1 spool of Pearl Crown Rayon thread, gold

1" wide velvet or satin ribbon for outer edge of needlepoint, white or your color choice

Sewing thread to match the ribbon

2 yards of 4" bullion fringe, peach, or any coordinating color

Sewing thread to match the bullion fringe

1/2 yard of plain cotton, or a drapery type such as damask, fabric for backing, any coordinating color

Two 19" squares of muslin for pillow insert

Stuffing

* A piece of crewel embroidery may be substituted.

This handsome pillow is designed around a piece of antique needlepoint—a classic piece of Victoriana with its cattail and bug subject matter—that turned up as I browsed through stacks of textiles at an antiques mall. Some of the variegated red background was missing, so with matching wool I reworked the missing areas.

The bug in the needlepoint is the one that is graphed and ready for cross-stitch embroidery in featured needleart on page 22.

The color palette chosen for this pillow includes the muted peach and off-white fabrics used in the Throw, with the additions of black, and burgundy.

1. Center the needlepoint on the muslin foundation and pin. Patch the remainder of the foundation according to instructions for the Antique Method on page 8, trimming the patches near to the edge of the worked area of the needlepoint. Baste the patches in place, then baste around the entire piece.

2. Embroider along patch seams in Single Feather Stitch (page 12) in gold Pearl Crown Rayon thread. Work the stitch so it adequately secures the patches.

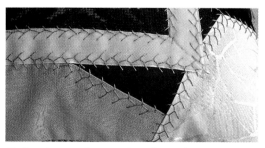

Embroidery stitching on the pillow is kept simple.

3. Beginning and ending at one corner, pin the ribbon along the edges of the needlepoint, covering the edges of both the needlepoint and the patches. Miter each corner, and finish the ends neatly. Baste. Work Single Feather Stitch along inner and outer edges of the ribbon.

4. Baste the fringe to the pillow the same as for the Throw. See step 4 on page 24.

5. Cut two pieces of backing fabric each 13" x 19". Hem one of the short ends of each by folding under twice and stitching. Place each with right sides together on the pillow, having the hemmed ends overlap at the center. Pin. Sew around. Turn the pillow right side out.

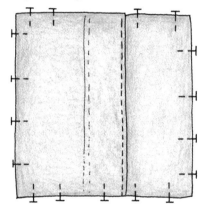

6. To make the insert, sew the two 19" squares of muslin together leaving an opening about 6" long. Turn the insert right side out. Pack stuffing into the insert until it is the firmness desired. Slip-stitch the opening closed. Place the insert inside the pillow.

Drapery Tiebacks

A crazy quilted tieback secures a lace curtain.

Materials
(fabrics are 44" wide)

The fabric amounts given below will make up to four tiebacks.

Paper, ruler, pencil
3/4 yard 100-percent cotton muslin for foundation
3/4 yard crinoline or stiff interfacing
3/4 yard of a plain cotton, or a drapery type such as damask, fabric for backing, any
    coordinating color
Fabrics for patches: same as those used for the Fringed Throw, plus black and burgundy
YLI Basting & Bobbin thread
1 spool of Pearl Crown Rayon thread, gold
3 yards of 4" bullion fringe, peach, or any coordinating color
Sewing thread to match the bullion fringe
Bone rings, 2 per tieback

1/2" seam allowance is used for assembly.

1. Tape sheets of paper together if necessary. Use the ruler and pencil to draw the pattern to the size indicated by the diagram. Seam allowances are included in the dimensions.

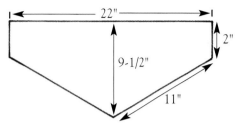

2. Cut one each of muslin, crinoline, and backing for each tieback, cutting along the straight grain of the fabric.

3. Patch the muslin foundation according to instructions for the Antique Method on page 8.

4. Embroider along patch seams in Single Feather Stitch (see page 12) in gold Pearl Crown Rayon thread.

5. Baste the crinoline to the wrong side of the patched and embroidered muslin.

6. Pin the fringe to the diagonal edges of the tieback with right sides together. Make a fold in the header of the fringe to fit the point of the tieback. Stop short of the seam allowance at each end. Baste.

7. With right sides together, pin the backing to the tieback. Sew, leaving an opening at the top to turn, taking care to avoid stitching the fringe ends into the seam. Trim seams, turn right side out, and press. Slipstitch the opening closed. Hand sew a bone ring to each upper corner of the tieback.

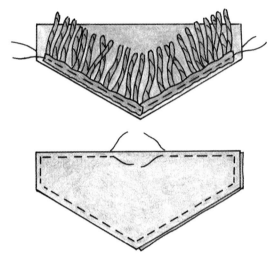

Showpiece Wall Quilt

Size: 50" x 62" not including the lace edging.

The Showpiece Wall Quilt displays antique textiles, giving it an old-fashioned air.

Embroidery melds a crazy quilt. It softens the angularity of patch edges and the juxtaposed fabrics and colors, transforming the quilt into a unified whole.

Work at least two rows of embroidery along each of the patch seams. Stitch a clothing label or a lace motif onto a patch and surround it with embroidery. Splash silk ribbon florals across patches. Embroider your initials and the date. Embroidery should be added until the piece seems complete.

This quilt displays some of my antique finds. To make a similar quilt you will need to assemble a collection of things, making the quilt when you have enough to use. The materials listing below includes the things I have found. Substitute items that you are able to collect.

Add a rod pocket to the back of the quilt, and display it on a north-facing wall, where it will receive no sunlight. (Sunlight hastens the deterioration of textiles.)

See tips for making a similar quilt on page 33.

1. Place the center piece at the center of the muslin. Following instructions for the Antique Method on page 8, place the tobacco felts and other antiques first, then add patches around them until the foundation is covered. Add trimmings and laces into seams as desired, and baste lace motifs onto some of the patches. Turn under the edges of patches that overlap onto the center piece. Add the wide lace at the top of the center piece, placing its ends under patches.

Materials

Antiques and other "finds" such as:
    17" square antique painting on velvet for the center of the quilt
    22" length of 6" wide antique lace
    11"x17" lace table mat or doily
    Butterfly motif tobacco felts (those used here are approximately 8-1/2" x 5-1/2")
    Clothing labels

43" x 55" piece of 100-percent cotton muslin for foundation
Fabrics for patches: same as those used for the Fringed Throw adding some darker shades such as navy, teal, coral, and light green
Pieces of laces, lace motifs, woven braids and other trimmings (in addition to the antiques)
YLI Basting & Bobbin thread
Size 8 pearl cotton threads in 8 or more shades of peach, yellow, green, blue, gray, and others for embroidery and for tying the quilt
Pearl Crown Rayon thread, gold
4 mm silk ribbons (see Silk Ribbon Embroidery on page 68), assorted colors
Waste canvas, 6-strand embroidery floss, graphed cross-stitch motifs (see Cross-stitch Embroidery using waste canvas on page 22)
1-3/4 yards of 44" wide velveteen or other fabric for borders, deep blue
Sewing thread to match the border fabric
2 yards of 54" wide plain cotton fabric for backing, any coordinating color
6-1/2" yards of 4-1/4" wide handmade or purchased cotton lace, ecru (choose a lace that has both long edges finished such as cluny, Venice, or handmade lace such as crocheted, knitted, or bobbin lace)
100-percent cotton sewing thread to match the 4-1/4" wide lace

1/2" seam allowance is used for assembly.

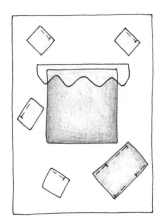

Collecting and Using Antique Textiles

Making a crazy quilt and including antique textiles is an excellent way of preserving and displaying the fabric pieces. When collecting antique textiles, look carefully to see that the piece is well enough intact so it will hold up to the handling it will receive. Do not cut up pieces that are in good condition. Pieces that have stains or torn areas or are otherwise too damaged to salvage may be cut up to be appliquéd or fastened onto a crazy quilt.

2. Embroider and embellish the quilt. Use gold Pearl Crown Rayon thread in a Double Feather Stitch around the center piece. Work cross-stitch motifs on some of the patches (see page 22). Work silk ribbon embroideries (see page 68) on some of the patches and along some seams. Fasten on lace motifs and other additions with embroidery stitches.

A piece of vintage lace in which darning was worked onto a net background.

The inner border of the Showpiece Wall Quilt features a line of embroidery in gold Pearl Crown Rayon thread to match that around the velvet center.

This butterfly print on flannel fabric once served as a premium given to the purchaser of a tobacco product.

3. Cut two side borders each 5" wide by the length of the quilt. Sew them on.

4. Cut top and bottom borders each 5" wide by the width of the quilt. Sew them on.

5. Cut the backing fabric to the same size as the quilt top and its borders. Pin the backing, right sides together, with the quilt top and sew around leaving an opening to turn. Turn right side out. Slip-stitch the opening closed.

6. With matching thread, invisibly hand-stitch the lace to the outer edge of the quilt. Gather the lace at each corner so it turns the corners smoothly.

7. Tie the quilt using size 8 pearl cotton and making ties on the back (see page 142). Add a rod pocket (see page 141).

Tips for Making a Similar Quilt

Before adding new, white lace motifs, "age" them by soaking in strong tea for an hour or longer. Remove from the tea, wash gently and rinse thoroughly. Allow to dry, press and use.

Choose some embroidery threads and embellishments to blend in with surrounding fabrics, and others to contrast.

Home decor trimmings are often in muted shades that blend into most color schemes. Choose those that can be sewn easily (some are too heavy for this purpose). Choose from gimpes, woven braids, and others.

Use a wide variety of embroidery stitches, consulting *The Magic of Crazy Quilting* for ideas.

Use 4 mm silk ribbon for some of the patch seam embroidery. Silk ribbon embroidery instructions appear on page 68.

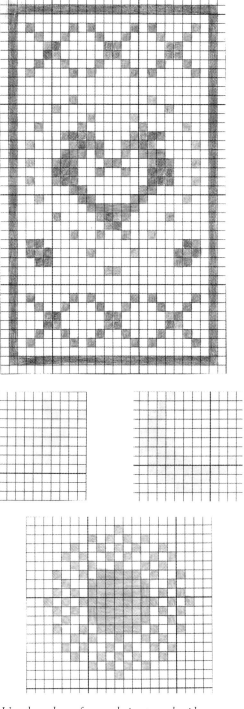

Use the colors of your choice to embroider these cross stitch designs.

Details of the Showpiece Quilt, displaying some of the many ways a crazy quilt can be embroidered and embellished.

Try to add something to every patch of the crazy quilt, and let some embroidery motifs "spill" onto adjoining patches.

Small cross-stitch motifs are worked into or appliquéd onto crazy patches. To appliqué a motif, cut out a previously worked cross-stitch design, press the edges under about 1/4", and slipstitch in place. Work embroidery around the motif.

Cross-stitched stars become shooting stars by embroidering lines behind them.

A mini-sampler is cross-stitched onto a crazy patch with silk ribbon roses added to the corners.

The little cross-stitched tree is a motif taken from a larger sampler design.

Cross-stitch, lace motifs, and silk ribbon embroidery decorate patches.

A patriotic ribbon, a clothing label, and silk ribbon embroidery decorate an area of the quilt.

Chapter 2

Fine Dining

Shades of gold offer a luxurious appearance in this set featuring Victorian-style fans.

Shadow-Work Embroidery

Large Victorian-style fans are a repeated motif in this dining room set. Make the set in the color scheme of your choice. I have chosen gold, a color that seems to say "opulence."

Limiting the colors is a way of simplifying a project. The dining room set is based on only four fabrics: the valance and runner are made of those four, while several additional fabrics are added to the quilt. Embroidery threads are kept simple also; the valance features only two colors, and the runner has four. The wall quilt goes a step beyond, featuring Shadow Work, Silk Ribbon and other embroideries.

For extra sturdiness and for accuracy in piecing the fans, some of the fabrics are backed with lightweight fusible interfacing. Follow instructions for the individual projects below. The four inch tassels added to each of the pieces are optional.

Projects:

Fan Valance

Table Runner

Inverted Arches Wall Quilt

Materials

100-percent cotton organdy
   fabric, white
6-strand cotton embroidery floss, white
Pencil
Size 26 tapestry needle
4" round embroidery hoop

Shadow-Work Embroidery

Shadow Work embroidery is very easy to do, and consists of the Closed Herringbone Stitch hand-embroidered onto the back of a semi-sheer fabric. The individual stitches are tiny in order to create a nearly solid effect in filling in the design that shows through to the front as a soft, shadowy effect. The edges of the Closed Herringbone Stitch form a double row of stitches on the front of the work, appearing exactly like backstitching (see the Outline/Reversed Backstitch Stitch on page 14). In addition to the Herringbone, the Reversed Backstitch is worked along any plain lines of the design.

Organdy fabric made of 100-percent cotton is the easiest type of semi-sheer fabric to use for shadow work. A stiffener in it makes it easy to trace and embroider a de-

Shadow work is fine embroidery, but easy to do.

sign. Other fabrics such as 100-percent cotton batiste, lightweight semi-sheer silks, or handkerchief linen may be used instead.

Suitable designs for shadow work consist of shapes to be filled in. You can create your own by drawing simple flowers and leaves such as the example shown. Many design ideas, including some of those shown on the pieces of the dining room set, are available as iron-on transfers in my book, *Shadow Work Embroidery*, Dover Publications, 1999.

1. Place the organdy over the diagram of the motif, and lightly trace the motif, using a fine pencil line that can be covered by the stitches, directly onto the organdy. You will be working on the reverse side of the piece. Place the organdy into the embroidery hoop with the pencil lines facing up.

2. Thread the tapestry needle with one or two strands of embroidery floss (one strand requires very tiny stitches, while two fills in the design more quickly). Begin the Closed Herringbone Stitch, leaving about a 1" tail and work the first few stitches over it. See page 14 for stitch instructions.

3. Begin at one end of a shape, keeping the stitches very short. The shorter the stitch, the more "filled in" the design will appear. To fill in narrow shapes, the stitches can be made longer than those in wider areas.

Work progressively from one end to the other, filling in the shape completely. An unbroken outline on the right side of the work should be visible when finished.

If the design has straight lines in it, work Reversed Backstitch (see page 14) along them. Sometimes a wide shape will have a line down the middle of it, such as the central vein of a leaf. This can be filled in by working one half of the leaf in

Closed Herringbone, then working the remaining half in the same stitch, but instead of piercing the fabric again at the center of the leaf, work into the stitches made for the first half. Or, if the area is more narrow, work the central line first in Reversed Backstitch, then fill in the leaf with Closed Herringbone.

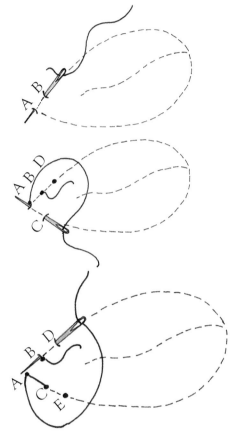

Fasten off threads by weaving the thread into the stitches, and then cutting the thread.

Continue to fill shapes and backstitch along lines until the design is completed. Do not run threads from one shape to another, as the stranding will show on the front.

4. Press the finished piece face down on a padded surface.

Motif for Shadow Work Embroidery

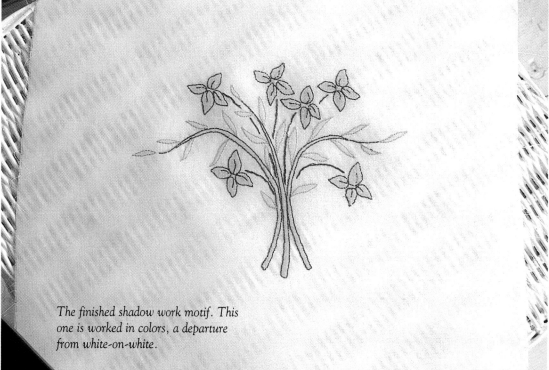

The finished shadow work motif. This one is worked in colors, a departure from white-on-white.

Fan Valance

This valance will fit a window frame from about 42" wide up to 52" wide.

A fan valance is elegant on its own, or can be installed over curtains.

Materials
(fabrics are 44" wide)

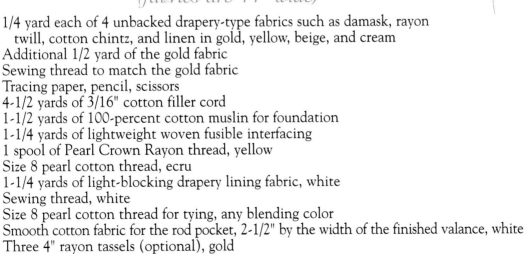

1/4 yard each of 4 unbacked drapery-type fabrics such as damask, rayon
   twill, cotton chintz, and linen in gold, yellow, beige, and cream
Additional 1/2 yard of the gold fabric
Sewing thread to match the gold fabric
Tracing paper, pencil, scissors
4-1/2 yards of 3/16" cotton filler cord
1-1/2 yards of 100-percent cotton muslin for foundation
1-1/4 yards of lightweight woven fusible interfacing
1 spool of Pearl Crown Rayon thread, yellow
Size 8 pearl cotton thread, ecru
1-1/4 yards of light-blocking drapery lining fabric, white
Sewing thread, white
Size 8 pearl cotton thread for tying, any blending color
Smooth cotton fabric for the rod pocket, 2-1/2" by the width of the finished valance, white
Three 4" rayon tassels (optional), gold

   Use a 1/4" seam allowance unless otherwise specified. Follow manufacturer's instructions to apply the fusible interfacing.

40

Preparation

1. Begin with an installed curtain rod. To have the valance atop a curtain, use a double rod. For a valance by itself, use a single rod. Consult with your local hardware dealer for installation instructions if needed.

2. Cut 5-1/2 yards of bias strips, 1-1/2" wide (see Bias Binding on page 139), out of the 1/2 yard of gold fabric. Sew the strips together. With 4-1/2 yards of the bias, make welting according to instructions on page 142. Set aside the remaining 1 yard.

Fan: make one for each valance.

1. With tracing paper, pencil and scissors, trace and cut out the Valance Fan Blade pattern and the Valance Fan Center pattern.

2. Cut out eight fan blades from the four fabrics using the Fan Blade pattern. Iron fusible interfacing onto the back of each blade. Arrange the colors any way you like, and with right sides together, machine sew together two of the fan blades. Press the seam open. Sew on another blade, press, and repeat until 8 blades are sewn together.

3. Sew welting to the rounded edge of the fan center, trim and clip the seam. Press the seam to the back. Place the fan center onto the fan and pin. Fasten the

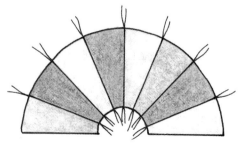

center to the fan by stitching in the ditch (stitch on top of the welting seam).

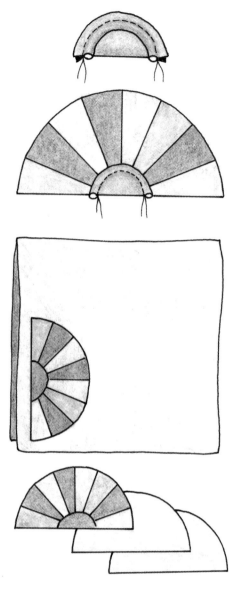

Assemble the valance

1. Using the assembled fan as a pattern, lay it onto the muslin and cut two pieces of muslin the same. Iron fusible interfacing onto the back of both pieces of muslin.

2. Measure the length of the curtain rod including the curved ends (see the diagram). Lay the fan and the two muslin pieces onto a flat surface, overlapping as

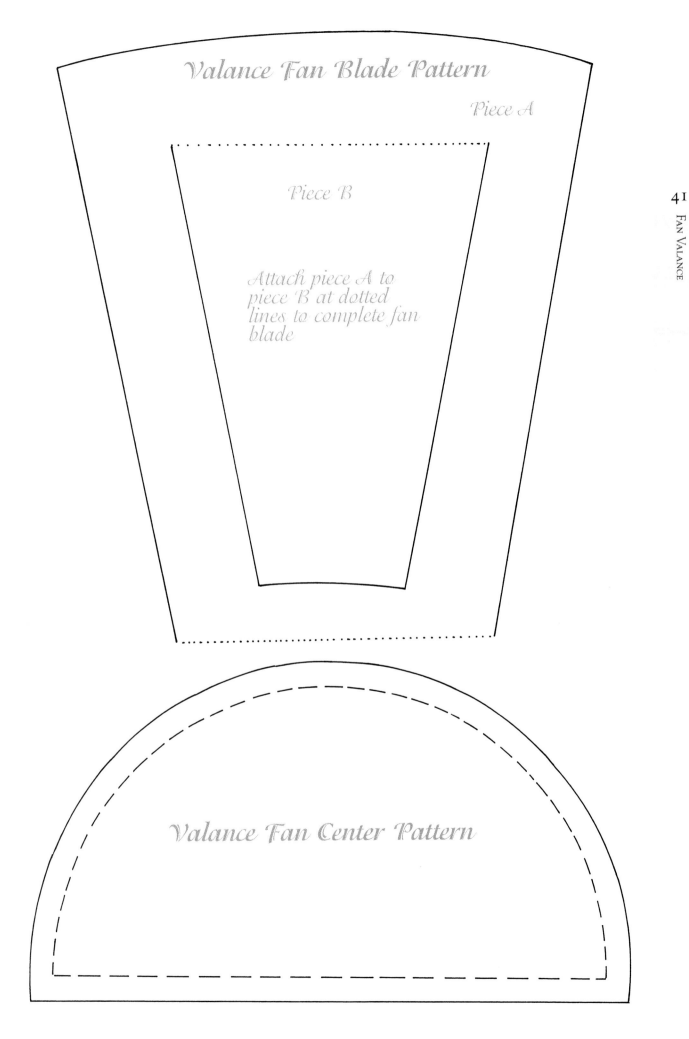

Valance Fan Blade Pattern

Piece A

Piece B

Attach piece A to piece B at dotted lines to complete fan blade

Valance Fan Center Pattern

shown to form the valance, and pin. The amount of overlap will depend on the measurement of the rod. Make the valance 1" longer than the rod measurement. Trim away the excess at the sides making sure to cut the ends straight. Flip the valance over and trim away the excess muslin behind the fan, retaining a seam allowance of about 1".

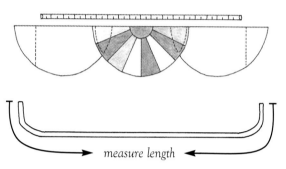

measure length

3. Unpin, and crazy patch the muslin sections following instructions for the Antique Method (see page 8) using the four patch fabrics. Embroider along the patch seams using Pearl Crown Rayon thread in meandering Outline Stitch. Work Lazy Daisy stitches along the Outline stitch. With ecru pearl cotton, embroider French Knots at intervals along the seams.

4. Sew welting to the curved edge of the fan, and to the outer curved edge of each side piece. Press the seams to the back.

Embroidery along patch seams is worked in Pearl Crown Rayon and pearl cotton threads on the Fan Valance.

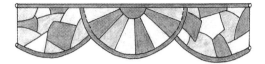

5. Place the three sections together, overlapping the fan onto the side pieces. Be sure the upper edge is straight across. Pin. Sew the pieces together by stitching in the ditch of the fan welting seam. Baste welting to the upper edge of the valance.

6. Lay the valance onto the light-blocking lining fabric with right sides together. Using the valance as a pattern, cut out the backing adding a seam allowance of at least 1/4" all around. Pin with right sides together to the upper edge, then machine-sew through all layers. Turn the backing to the back and press. Lay the piece on a flat surface and fold and press under the seam allowances of all curved edges. Slipstitch in place.

To neat-finish the ends of the valance, using the bias that was set aside earlier, cut four pieces each 1" longer than each end of the valance. With right sides together, sew one to each end through all layers. Press the bias to the back, fold under and slipstitch over the seam, folding in the raw ends for a neat finish.

7. Tie the layers of the valance using one strand of size 8 pearl cotton. Place the ties in seam allowances where they won't show on the front, making the ties on the back; see page 142.

8. Make a rod pocket following the instructions on page 141, with the 2-1/2" wide fabric. Sew the tassels to the valance as shown in the photograph (optional). Slide the valance onto the curtain rod.

Table Runner

Size: 15" wide by the desired length. If a drop is desired, add 26" to the measurement of the table to have a 13" drop at each end (not including the tassels).

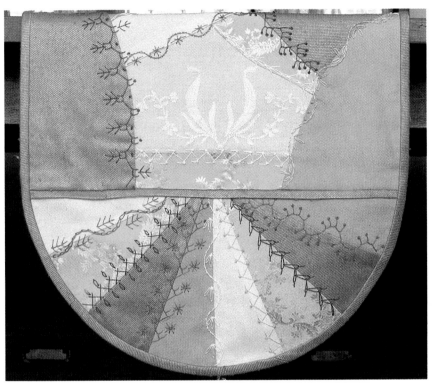

The Table Runner can be made to either fit the top of the table, or to drape at each end.

Materials

Medium-weight 100-percent cotton fabric for the foundation, 15" by the desired length of the runner, gold

1/4 yard each of 4 unbacked drapery-type fabrics as used for the valance in gold, yellow, beige, and cream

Additional 1/2 yard of the gold fabric

Sewing thread to match the gold fabric

Organdy fabric, 6-strand embroidery floss, 6 or more drawings or transfer designs (see Shadow Work Embroidery on page 36)

Tracing paper, pencil, scissors

1/4 yard of lightweight woven fusible interfacing

Size 8 pearl cotton threads for embroidery, white and three shades of gold

Backing fabric, 15" wide by the length of the runner, any coordinating color

Two 4" rayon tassels (optional), gold

1/4" seam allowances

The foundation fabric in this project is a medium shade of gold. This is to better highlight the Shadow Work motifs. A large Shadow Work motif is placed at the center of the runner. Instead of the welting as used in the valance, bias is cut to make bindings. Use the fusible interfacing for the fans, but not for the remainder of the runner.

Decide on a length for the runner; it can be made to fit the top of the table only, or to have a 13" drop at each end. Measure to find the total length of the runner.

1. Decide on the total length of the runner, and subtract 14" from this (the total of the fan ends), then add 1/2" for seam allowances. Cut the gold foundation fabric 15" wide by this length.

2. Work crazy quilting on the gold cotton foundation fabric using the four patch and fan fabrics, and the Shadow Work motifs for some of the patches. Follow instructions for the Antique Method of crazy patching (page 8).

This shadow work motif is available as an iron-on transfer in my book, Shadow Work Embroidery, *Dover Publications.*

3. With tracing paper and pencil, trace and cut out the Runner Fan Blade pattern.

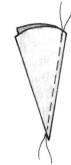

4. Cut 16 fan blades, four each of the four patch and fan fabrics. Iron fusible interfacing onto the back of each. Arranging the colors any way you like, place two fan blades with right sides together and sew them together. Press the seam open. Sew on another blade, press, and repeat until 8 blades are sewn together. Repeat to make a second fan.

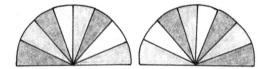

5. Out of the gold fabric cut 1-1/4" wide bias (see Bias Binding, page 139). Cut 2-1/2 yards plus twice the length of the runner. Sew the pieces together to make one length.

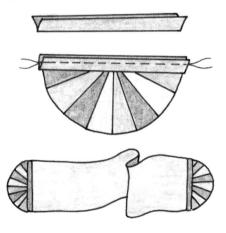

6. Cut off two 15" lengths of the bias for flanges. Fold them in half lengthwise with wrong sides together. Machine-baste one flange to each straight end of each fan matching raw edges. Sew one fan to each end of the patched foundation through all layers. Press the flanges toward the fan blades.

7. Embroider along the patch seams and the seams of the fans, using pearl cotton threads and the stitches of your choice.

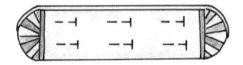

8. Lay the embroidered runner, wrong sides together, with the backing fabric and pin. Cut the backing fabric the same as the runner.

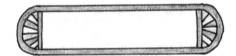

9. With right sides together, sew the bias to the outer edge of the runner. (See Applying Bias Edging using the Sew 'n Slipstitch Method on page 140.) Tie the layers of the runner using 1 strand of size 8 Pearl Cotton. Place the ties in seam allowances where they won't show on the front. Make the ties on the back. See page 142. Sew a tassel to each end of the runner (optional).

Runner Fan Blade Pattern

Inverted Arches Wall Quilt

Size: 38-1/2" wide x 48" long, not including tassel.

A crazy quilt made in an interesting shape will draw attention in any room.

The large fan of the valance is repeated in the wall quilt.

The fabrics, threads, and embellishments to be used on a quilt will depend on what you are able to find, and what you have already collected. The ingredients as given for this quilt include a hankie purchased at an antiques shop, Silk Ribbon and Shadow Work embroideries that are samples made while designing my two books published by Dover Publications, *Ribbon Embroidery* and *Shadow Work Embroidery*. You can make and collect small embroideries also, making a quilt when you have a quantity of them.

Architecture can inspire the shape or form of a quilt. This window, turned upside down, suggests the shape of the Inverted Arches Wall Quilt.

Materials

1 yard of medium-weight 100-percent cotton fabric for the foundations, gold
1/4 yard each of 4 unbacked drapery-type fabrics as used for the valance in gold, yellow, beige, and cream
Additional 1/2 yard of the cream fabric
Sewing thread to match the cream fabric
Several additional patching fabrics in colors to blend and contrast (I added black, yellow, brown, dark green, and gold)
1/4 yard of fusible interfacing
Organdy fabric, 6-strand embroidery floss, 6 or more drawings or transfer designs (see Shadow Work Embroidery on page 36)
Purchased or self-made hankie or doily for the center of the quilt
Venice cotton lace, sufficient amount for edging the hankie or doily (if needed)
Any desired sew-on trims and laces
Size 8 pearl cotton threads in assorted colors that contrast with the patch fabrics
4 mm silk ribbons (see Silk Ribbon Embroidery on page 68), assorted colors
6-1/4 yards of 3/16" cotton filler cord
1-1/2 yards of smooth cotton fabric for backing, any coordinating color
6" x 38-1/2" piece of fabric for the rod pocket, same as for the backing
Three 4" rayon tassels (optional), gold

1/4" seam allowances are used for assembly

1. Make 7-1/2 yards of 1-1/2" wide bias out of the cream fabric following instruction for Bias Binding on page 139. Out of the bias, make 6-1/4 yards of welting (see page 142), reserving the remaining bias for binding.

2. Make one fan according to instructions on page 40, following steps 1-3, and using the cream welting.

3. Make 6 or more Shadow Work embroideries following instructions on page 36.

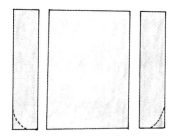

4. Cut three foundations out of the gold cotton fabric: a rectangle 27" wide x 35 1/2" long for the quilt center, and two side pieces each 6-1/2" wide by 35-1/2" long. Cut one bottom corner of each of the two side pieces in a curve.

5. Patch the gold foundation fabrics according to instructions for the Antique Method (page 8) placing the doily or hankie at the middle of the quilt center. Use the shadow work embroideries as some of the patches. Add laces into some of the seams.

6. Embroider along patch seams using hand-embroidery stitches (pages 11-15).

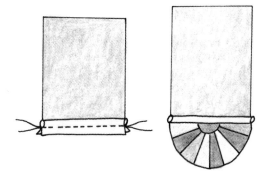

Embellish, adding silk ribbon motifs (see instructions for Silk Ribbon Embroidery on page 68).

7. Baste welting to the bottom edge of the quilt center. Pin the large fan with right sides together over the welting, and sew along the seam of the welting. Open and press.

Work hand embroidery along the seams of the fan blades using the pearl cotton in the colors and stitches of your choice.

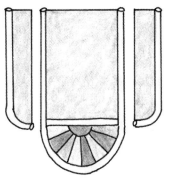

8. Sew one length of welting around both sides and the bottom of the quilt center beginning and ending at each of the upper edges. Clip seams at the corners.

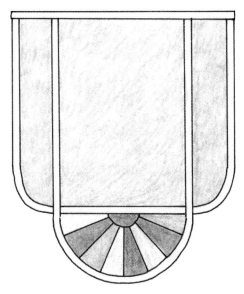

9. Sew welting to the outer curved edge of each side piece. Press the seams toward the quilt. With right sides together, sew the side pieces to the quilt.

10. Place the backing fabric wrong sides together with the quilt top and cut to make it 1/4" to 1/2" larger than the quilt. Pin throughout. On the back of the quilt, fold in the seam allowances all around and pin. Slipstitch the backing to the quilt. Tie the quilt (see page 142) making the ties on the back.

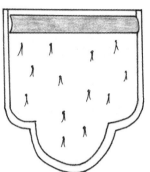

11. Add a binding to the upper edge using the remainder of the 7-1/2 yards of the bias (see Applying Bias Edging using the Sew 'n Slipstitch Method on page 140). Add a rod pocket to the upper edge of the back following instructions on page 141. Sew on the tassels as shown in the photograph (optional).

Details of the Inverted Arches Wall Quilt, displaying some of the ways a crazy quilt can be embroidered and embellished.

At the quilt's center, a vintage hankie is edged with Venice lace and embroidered with silk ribbon.

An embroidered spider web is a feature of many Victorian crazy quilts.

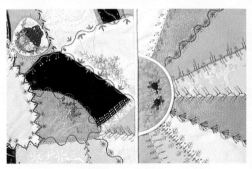

Use a variety of thread colors for embroidery along the patch seams of a crazy quilt.

Shadow work and other motifs make this quilt unique.

Chapter 3

A Tea Set

Getting ready for tea on the summer porch.

Featured Needleart:
Battenberg Lace-Making

The combination of blue and white always seems to brighten up a room. Confetti piecing provides a crisp contrast to the soft curves of Battenberg lace in this set that is sure to become a favorite.

Battenberg lace-making is easy to learn. The lace tape is formed into shapes, then tacked with pearl cotton thread and lacy fillers are added as you go along. You will find the process goes quickly after you learn how.

Use Battenberg lace for edgings, doilies, and motifs. These can be placed onto a crazy quilt as it is being patched and embellished. Simply tack them onto the patches either with sewing stitches, or with embroidery such as French Knots.

A Battenberg motif fastened onto a crazy quilt with embroidery stitches.

Projects:

Tea cozy

Battenberg Table Mat

Placemat

Potholder

Battenberg Lace-Making

Battenberg lace is easy to make by using specially made lace tapes. Lace tapes are woven to include a pull thread along one or both edges so they can easily be shaped. Although picot-edged tape is used here, plain-edged tapes may also be used. The lace tape is laid directly onto a paper pattern and pinned into place as it is shaped. It is then secured by fastening on a thread such as pearl cotton and using it to tack the overlapped edges and create small lacy fillers.

Try the patterns given here, and once you've learned how, try drawing designs of your own and working lace onto them. There is an endless variety in the motifs and edgings that can be devised by forming loops, curves, folds, and other shapes.* Once you've drawn a design on paper, estimate the amount of lace tape needed by following the design with a string. Then, measure the string to determine the yardage.

To make Battenberg lace you will need a padded ironing board cover or other thickly padded surface that can be pinned into (an iron is not needed). The pins must be pushed in so the heads do not interfere with the hand tacking and the working of the fillers.

The following instructions are for making the Large Battenberg Motif. Make the Small Battenberg Motif the same way, but use one yard of lace tape per motif, and make only one tracing of the pattern in this book, then make additional copies as needed—one per motif.

*An excellent book of designs for Battenberg edgings, motifs, and larger pieces is *Battenberg and Other Tape Laces, Techniques, Stitches and Designs*, by The Butterick Publishing Company, 1988, Dover Publications, Inc., Mineola, N.Y.

Pinning a Battenberg motif on the ironing board.

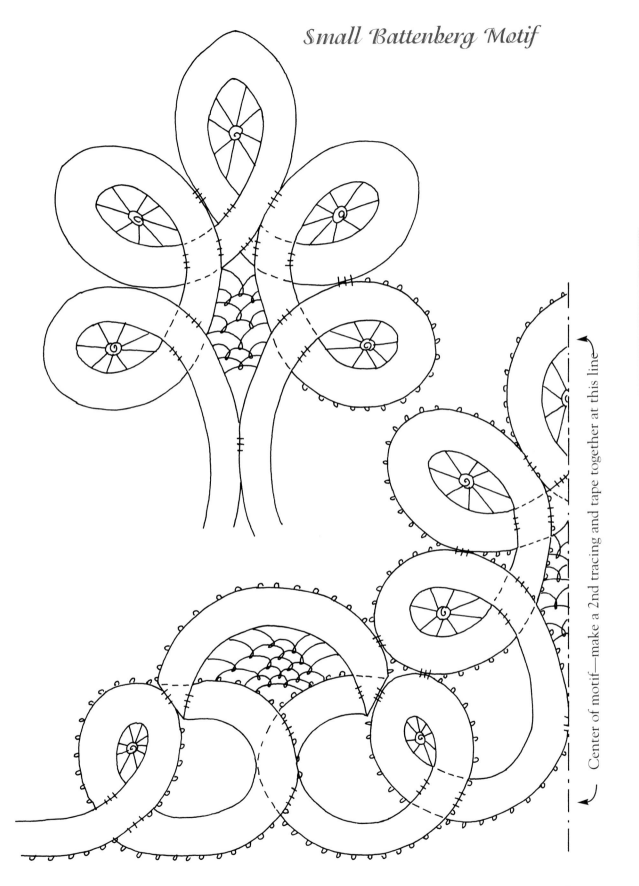

Small Battenberg Motif

Center of motif—make a 2nd tracing and tape together at this line

Large Battenberg Motif

Materials and tools

2-1/4 yards of 8 mm picot-edged Battenberg lace tape, white
1 spool of size 12 pearl cotton, white
Pins
Tapestry needle, size 26
Artist's tracing paper and a pencil
Ironing board with padded cover

54

1. Trace the Large Battenberg Motif pattern from this book making two tracings and taping them together at the center line to complete the motif, then make as many additional tracings as needed. You will need one for each motif that you are making. Begin with the 2-1/4 yards of lace tape and do not cut the tape; it should be in one piece for the entire motif.

2. Locate the pull thread in the edge of the end of the lace tape: it is a heavier thread than others in the tape. Pull up on the thread while gathering the lace tape until about 12" of the thread is pulled out, and also pull some gathers from the opposite end of the tape to avoid losing the pull thread. Push the gathers along as you work, keeping them just beyond where you are working. When you run out of gathers to use in shaping the tape, pull from the other end, bringing the gathers up to where you are working.

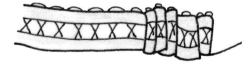

3. Pin the traced pattern to the ironing board. You will be working on the wrong side of the lace. Begin laying the lace tape at one end of the pattern, shaping it to fit exactly inside the lines of the pattern. Pin as you shape, and push the excess gathers

along, placing sufficient gather into the curves so they lie smoothly, and folding the tape where indicated on the pattern. Push the pins in until the heads are even with the lace tape. Complete the Motif, adding as many pins as needed to hold the curves.

4. Begin at the end at which you began laying the tapes earlier. Thread the tapestry needle with a working length of the Pearl Cotton, perhaps 30" or so. Fasten on the pearl cotton with several tiny stitches close together where the first overlap is indicated on the pattern. Bring the thread ("bring the thread," means carrying the thread if only a short distance, otherwise taking a few tiny stitches along the way) to the first Spider Web Filler. Work the Filler as described below. Bring the thread to the next overlapped, butted, or folded area, and tack with a few stitches. Continue, tacking the tapes where needed, and working Fillers as you come to them. When the thread is used up, end with several tiny stitches on an overlap, then begin a new thread, and continue. When the Motif is complete, remove pins and press.

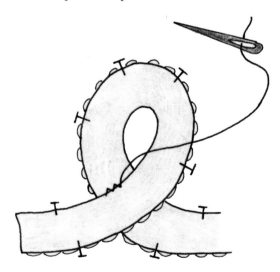

Lace Fillings

Scalloped Filler

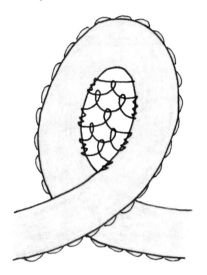

This stitch is worked in the same way as the Buttonhole Stitch. Make a straight stitch going across the opening, then bring the thread down the side of the opening with a few small stitches. Make a stitch the same way as the Buttonhole Stitch (see page 11), working the stitch over the straight stitch instead of through fabric, then fasten the thread at the opposite side of the opening. Continue, working downwards and making stitches as needed, increasing or decreasing the looped stitches to fit the space.

Spider Web Filler

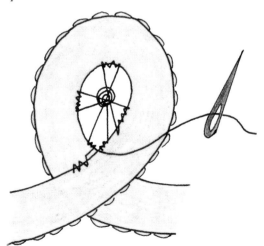

To create spokes, stitch back and forth across the opening as shown in the diagram. Then, do not fasten off, but begin weaving for several rounds over and under each spoke. Fasten off with a few stitches into the weaving itself, then stitch into the lace tape, and continue on.

Objects such as this antique rug beater may suggest ideas for designing Battenberg motifs.

Tea Cozy

Size: 13" wide by 10" high.

The tea cozy keeps a pot warm on the porch railing.

Materials

Tracing paper, plain paper, pencil, scissors

1 - 2 cuts of:

    1/4 yard length each of 8 different quilting cotton fabrics including prints with medium to royal blue backgrounds, light blue prints on white backgrounds, and solids in white and blue (see Confetti Piecing instructions on page 15)

100-percent cotton sewing thread to blend with the fabrics, also dark blue and white

2-1/4 yards of 8 mm picot-edged Battenberg lace tape, white

Size 12 pearl cotton

8" x 14" piece of white fabric

1/2 yard of dark blue fabric for the bias bindings and flanges (Note: if making the entire tea set, 1/2 yard is sufficient for all of the projects)

11" x 27" piece of high-loft poly batting

1/4" seam allowances

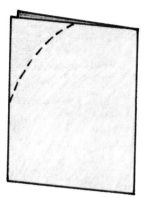

1. Make a paper pattern by taping and cutting the plain paper to make a rectangle 13" wide by 10" high. (The seam allowances are included in these dimensions.) To make the upper edges match, fold the paper in half lengthwise and draw a rounded edge at the upper corner. Cut along the drawn line. Open the paper.

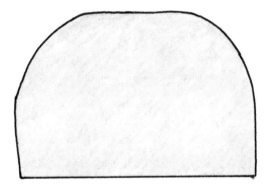

2. Following instructions on page 15, work Confetti Piecing to make two pieces, each about 13" x 10-1/2".

3. Use the paper pattern to cut two pieces of Confetti the same. Also cut two of batting, and two of lining fabric.

4. Trace and cut out the Inset pattern on page 58. Cut one inset out of the white fabric. Make one Large Battenberg Motif following instructions for Battenberg Lace-Making on page 54. Center the Battenberg Motif onto the inset keeping the top and bottom edges inside the seam allowances. Pin, and machine sew using white thread along both long edges of the lace tape to secure the lace to the fabric.

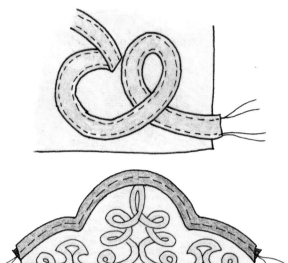

5. To make the flange, cut dark blue bias strips 1" wide by 18" long (see Bias Binding instructions on page 139). Fold the bias in half lengthwise and press. Machine-baste the flange to the upper edge of the inset with right sides together.

Press the seam to the back.

6. Lay the inset onto one of the Confetti pieces aligning bottom edges. Pin. Stitch in the ditch (see page 140) along the basting line of the flange. On the back, trim away the excess Confetti behind the flange, retaining a 1/4" seam allowance. (Reserve the Confetti for making the Potholder, see page 64.)

7. Layer the following in the same order, matching all edges, and pin:

Confetti backing, face down,
One piece of batting,
The 2 lining pieces, right sides together,
One piece of batting,
The Confetti and inset front, right side up.

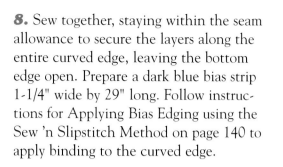

8. Sew together, staying within the seam allowance to secure the layers along the entire curved edge, leaving the bottom edge open. Prepare a dark blue bias strip 1-1/4" wide by 29" long. Follow instructions for Applying Bias Edging using the Sew 'n Slipstitch Method on page 140 to apply binding to the curved edge.

9. Pin the three layers of the bottom edge all around. Sew around, staying within the seam allowance to secure the layers. Prepare a dark blue bias strip 1-1/4" wide by 26" long, and bind the lower edge, using the Sew 'n Slipstitch Method.

Inset for Table Mat & Tea Cozy

Trace pattern twice and tape together along this line

Cutting line for Tea Cozy

Cutting line for Table Mat

Battenberg Table Mat

Size: 13" x 27".

Confetti piecing in blues and white makes a striking tablemat.

Materials

Tracing paper, pencil, scissors
4-1/2 yards of 8mm picot-edged Battenberg lace tape, white
Size 12 pearl cotton
Two pieces of white fabric each 14" x 7"
1 - 2 cuts of:
   1/4 yard length each of 8 different quilting cotton fabrics including prints with
   medium to royal blue backgrounds, light blue prints on white backgrounds, and
   solids in white and blue (see Confetti Piecing instructions on page 15)
100-percent cotton sewing thread to blend with the fabrics, also dark blue and white
1/2 yard of dark blue fabric for the bias binding and flanges (Note: if making the
   entire tea set, 1/2 yard is sufficient for all of the projects)
13" x 27" piece of high-loft poly batting
13" x 27" piece of cotton fabric for backing, any coordinating color
Size 8 pearl cotton, medium blue

1/4" seam allowances

1. Trace and cut out the Inset pattern on page 58. Use the pattern to cut two insets out of the white fabric. Make two Large Battenberg Motifs following instructions for Battenberg Lacemaking on page 52. Center one of the Battenberg lace pieces onto one of the insets keeping the top and bottom edges inside the seam allowances. Pin, and machine sew using white thread along both long edges of the lace tape to secure the lace to the fabric. Repeat to make the second inset.

2. Following instructions on page 15, work Confetti Piecing to make one piece 13" x 15".

3. Cut two dark blue bias strips each 1" wide by 13" long for the flanges (see Bias Binding instructions on page 139). Fold them in half lengthwise with wrong sides together. Baste one to each end of the 13" x 15" Confetti piece. Sew one inset

to each of the flanges. Press the flange toward the mat.

4. Using the sewn piece as a pattern, cut the backing fabric to match. Cut one of batting the same. Stack the layers: backing (face down), batting, then Confetti (right side up). Pin. Sew around the mat, staying within the seam allowance to secure the layers.

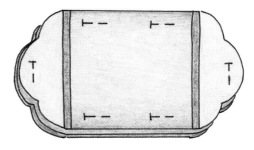

5. Prepare a dark blue bias strip 1-1/4" wide by 70" long, and follow instructions for Applying Bias Edging using the Sew 'n Slipstitch Method on page 140 to bind the outer edge of the mat. When sewing on the binding, make and sew a small fold (taking in about 1/4" of the bias) at the inward corners of the end scallops to enable the bias to fold smoothly to the back.

6. Finish the mat by tying the layers (see page 142), using the medium blue pearl cotton. Make the ties on the right side of the mat.

Placemat

Size: 17-1/2" x 12-1/2".

Make a set of placemats featuring two each of the Small Battenberg Motif.

Materials

Tracing paper, pencil, scissors
2 yards of 8 mm picot-edged Battenberg lace tape, white
Size 12 pearl cotton
2 pieces of white fabric, each 7" square
1 - 2 cuts of:
   1/4 yard length each of 8 different quilting cotton fabrics including prints with
   medium to royal blue backgrounds, light blue prints on white backgrounds, and
   solids in white and blue (see Confetti Piecing instructions on page 15)
100-percent cotton sewing thread to blend with the fabrics, also dark blue and white
1/2 yard of dark blue fabric for the bias binding and flanges (Note: if making the
   entire tea set, 1/2 yard is sufficient for all of the projects)
17-1/2" x 12-1/2" piece of high-loft poly batting
17-1/2" x 12-1/2" piece of cotton fabric for backing, any coordinating color
Size 8 pearl cotton, medium blue

1/4" seam allowances

Note: materials and instructions are per each placemat. Make the number of placemats needed for your place settings.

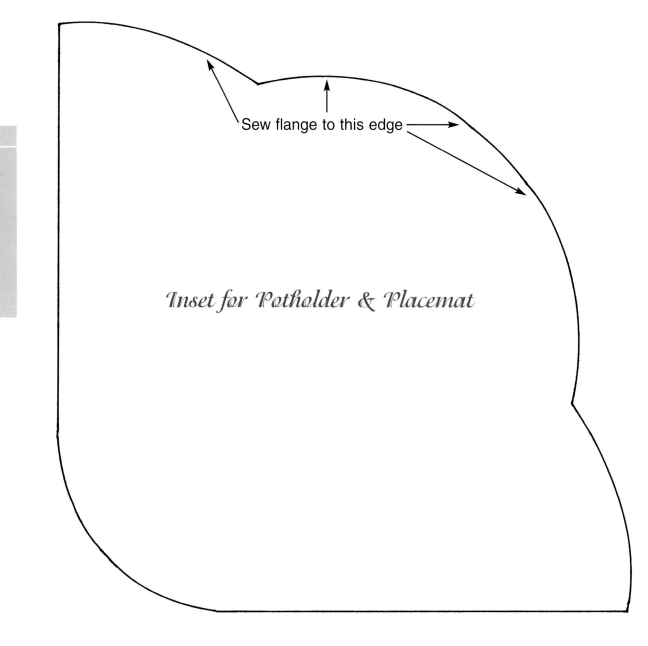

Sew flange to this edge

Inset for Potholder & Placemat

1. Trace and cut out the Inset pattern, opposite. Use the pattern to cut two insets out of the white fabric squares. Make two Small Battenberg Motifs following

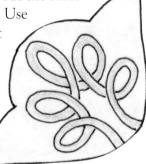

instructions for Battenberg Lace-Making on page 52. Center one of the motifs onto one of the insets. Pin, and machine sew using white thread along both long edges of the lace tape to secure the lace to the fabric. Repeat for the second inset.

2. Following instructions on page 15, work Confetti Piecing to make one piece 17-1/2" x 12-1/2".

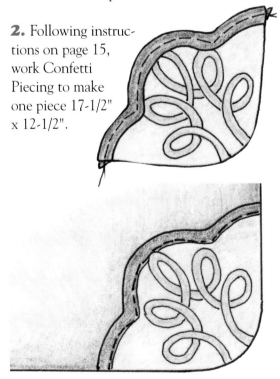

3. Cut two dark blue bias strips each 1" wide by 10-1/2" long for the flanges (see Bias Binding instructions on page 139). Fold them in half lengthwise with wrong sides together. Pin the flanges to the inner edges of each inset, matching raw edges. Place and pin the insets onto opposite corners of the Confetti piece. Cut all four corners of the Confetti piece rounded to match the outer edge of the inset. Sew on the insets, stitching in the ditch along the flange seams. Trim away excess Confetti from behind the insets, leaving a 1/4" seam allowance.

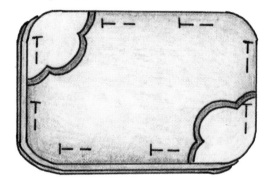

4. Using the sewn piece as a pattern, cut the backing fabric to match. Cut one of batting the same. Stack the layers: backing (face down), batting, Confetti (right side up). Pin. Sew around the mat, staying within the seam allowance to secure the layers.

5. Prepare a dark blue bias strip 1-1/4" wide by 58" long, and follow instructions for Applying Bias Edging using the Sew 'n Slipstitch Method on page 140 to bind the outer edge of the mat.

6. Finish the mat by tying the layers (see page 142) using the medium blue pearl cotton. Make the ties on the right side of the mat.

Potholders

Size: 8-1/2"square.

Use leftover pieces of confetti piecing to make attractive potholders.

Materials

8-1/2" Confetti pieced square

100-percent cotton sewing thread to blend with the fabrics, also dark blue and white

1 yard of 8 mm picot-edged Battenberg lace tape, white

Size 12 pearl cotton

7" square of white fabric

1/2 yard of dark blue fabric for the bias binding and flanges (Note: if making the entire tea set, 1/2 yard is sufficient for all of the projects)

8-1/2" square of 100-percent cotton batting (for extra protection you may want to use 2 layers of batting – cut 2 squares each 8-1/2"; place together and handle as one)

8-1/2" square of cotton backing fabric

Size 8 pearl cotton, medium blue or quilting thread in white or light blue

There may be Confetti'd pieces left over from the above projects sufficient to make one or two potholders. If not, one cut of the 8 fabrics will make about two potholders.

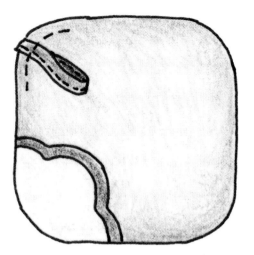

Follow instructions for the placemats, making the following changes per potholder: make one inset, making and using one Small Battenberg Motif. Cut dark blue bias strips 1" wide by 16" long for the flange, and 1-1/4" wide by 32" long for the bias edging. Make a loop: cut a 5" length of the 1" wide bias, fold the long edges to the center, and press. Fold again at the center and topstitch. Baste the loop to one corner of the potholder before the binding is added. To finish, tie the potholder with size 8 pearl cotton in medium blue, or use quilting thread and stitch-in-the-ditch by machine.

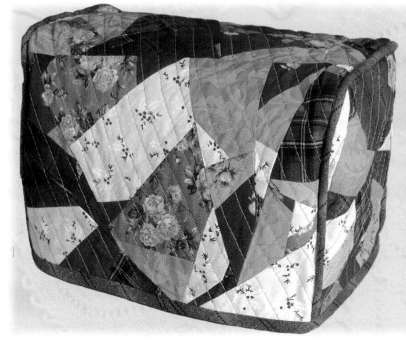

It is easy to make covers for appliances such as this toaster cover. Make one large piece of Confetti that fits over the appliance, then make two end pieces and sew them on. Add batting and backing to the Confetti pieces. To be sure of fitting the appliance properly, measure carefully, then sew up a sample using scrap fabric. Insert welting into the seams (see page 142) and finish the bottom edges with bias (see page 139). Quilt or tie.

Chapter 4
For the Gardener

This set allows you to enjoy the floral garden even when not in bloom.

Featured Needleart:

Silk Ribbon Embroidery

What's a gardener to do on a rainy day, or in winter? When it's not possible to be outdoors digging, pruning, planting and tending, you can still take notes, organize photos, or enjoy a framed memento.

Use the Antique Method of crazy quilting, and embroider silk ribbon florals to make a crazy quilted picture for year-round enjoyment. Begin with an interesting antique frame found in an attic, at a yard sale or antiques shop.

Fast Confetti piecing is used to make a matched set of removable book covers. Neatly edged in welting, with cloth ties to keep contents intact, these attractive covers are designed to be washable and durable. The inside flaps of the covers also provide handy storage for pencils, extra photos, negatives, or newspaper clippings. The covers are excellent gift ideas. Designed for year-round use, they will be treasured by any enthusiastic gardener. Although a garden set here, the covers can be made to fit any size notebook, photo book, or binder for any purpose.

Projects:

Framed Picture with Silk-Ribbon Embroidery

Garden Notebook Cover

Photo Log Cover

Antique Method Scrapbook Cover

Materials

4 mm silk ribbons, 2 mm and
    7 mm widths may also be used
Size 18 Chenille needle
Embroidery hoop, scissors

Silk ribbon embroidery is easy to do and produces results quickly.

Projects:

Silk Ribbon Embroidery

Of the many embroidery and embellishment methods, Silk Ribbon is my favorite. As a quick and easy way to "dress up" a crazy quilted project, use Silk-Ribbon Embroidery to do a few small motifs, or splash a larger one across a patch or two. Use it in place of thread to embroider along the edges of patches, or add silk ribbon stitches to a row of thread embroidery.

The regular embroidery stitches are used with the addition of the Ribbon Stitch. Because the ribbon is wider than thread, ribbon embroidery covers much more area than a similar length of thread, and that is why it seems to fill in so quickly. Because the stitches stand up from the fabric, they are shaded by the effect of light and shadow, eliminating the need to use additional shades of a color to assimilate a realistic effect.

A silk ribbon embroidery worked on Ladies and Fans, an all-silk crazy quilt (this quilt is featured in my book The Magic of Crazy Quilting).

Use only high quality silk ribbons. Silk ribbons made in Japan (the same as those packaged by YLI), are made in 2 mm, 4 mm, and 7 mm widths especially for embroidery. They are very easy to embroider with when a size 18 Chenille needle is used. This size needle pokes a hole through the fabric that is large enough for the ribbon to pass through easily. Although a smaller needle will also work, the ribbon will be subjected to more wear and tear. Using short lengths of ribbon also prevents fraying. If your ribbons are not flat and smooth, iron them using a dry iron on low heat.

An embroidery hoop is recommended. Use a hand-held hoop for smaller projects, and a 14" round lap hoop for quilt-size projects. Begin with a length of ribbon approximately 12" to 14" long.

Thread the needle by bringing the ribbon through the eye of the needle, then pierce the ribbon about 1/2" from the same end. Pull on the other end to settle the resulting "knot" into the needle's eye.

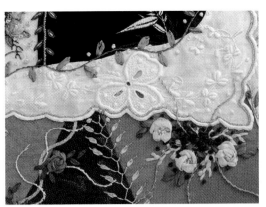

A detail of the Framed Picture showing silk ribbon work and other embroidery.

A scene such as this delightful window box combo can provide inspiration for a silk ribbon embroidery motif.

To begin, make a tiny stitch at the back of the work, and run the needle through to the front while piercing the tail of the stitch. To fasten off, make two or three tiny stitches on the back of the work.

The Ribbon Stitch is exclusive to ribbon embroidery. Lay the ribbon flat on the fabric, and bring the needle through at the desired length of the stitch. Watch the stitch form, and stop pulling when the stitch looks like a small leaf. A simple variation is to allow the ribbon to puff away from the fabric a little bit while making the stitch. These stitches make ideal small leaves, and can also be used for flower petals.

With the exception of the Ribbon Stitch, other embroidery stitches are made in the normal way. Experiment with the embroidery stitches to form floral and other embroideries. For silk ribbon motif ideas, consult my iron-on transfer book, *Ribbon Embroidery*, Dover Publications; 1997.

Here are some variations that can be done in silk ribbon:

Make French Knots winding the ribbon once, twice, or three or four times around the needle. Experiment by making some knots with the ribbon tightly wrapped, and others with the ribbon wound very loosely.

To form roses, work the Outline Stitch in a small circle, starting from the center working around until the rose is as full as you like it. One 14" length of ribbon makes a small rose; fasten on a second length and continue if you wish to make it larger.

Use Lazy Daisy Stitches to add leaves to the rose.

Making Straight Stitches by twisting the ribbon creates a narrow, twisted stitch that is useful for flower stems or daisy petals.

Framed Picture with Silk Ribbon Embroidery

Crazy quilting has many applications, including framed pieces such as this one.

Materials

Picture frame, antique or modern, in the size desired (the frame used here is 16" x 20")

Optional: have a mat cut to fit the frame, especially if glass will be used

Piece of foamcore to fit into the frame (available at a framer's shop)

100-percent cotton muslin for foundation, at least 4" larger than the frame in each direction

Pencil

Vintage embroidered fabric doily with a damaged center in a size that will fit within the area of the frame

Scraps of interesting fabrics – I used kimono pieces, silk/rayon damask, and some hand-dyed silks (see page 103 for hand dyeing silks)

Variety of metallic fibers (used here are Kreinik's 1/8" and 1/16" ribbons and #8 braid, and Japan Gold #5) in shades of gold

Hand sewing threads, silk or cotton, for couching the metallic fibers

4 mm and 7 mm silk ribbons in assorted colors

Silk Serica and Soie Perlee silk threads for embroidery along patch seams, your choice of colors

YLI Select Thread, or size 50 cotton sewing thread for lacing, any color

Collect the materials before beginning this project worked in the Antique Method of crazy patching. Begin with an interesting frame, an embroidered doily, and an assortment of scraps of interesting fabrics. To this add brilliant metallic gold and other colors in ribbons, braids and trimmings, or other materials of your choosing.

Note: In step 8 of the instructions below, if glass is used, the frame must have sufficient depth to accommodate two or more layers of mat board in addition to the glass.

1. Center the frame on the muslin and draw along the interior edge of the frame. This gives the outer boundary of the picture. If the picture will be matted, use the mat instead of the frame for this step.

Note: Be particular about both patching and embroidery in order to avoid "shrinkage" of the piece. This is caused by patches that do not lie flat, and by embroidery that pulls up and bunches the fabrics. Lay patches carefully, press the piece when necessary, and use an embroidery hoop for embroidery and embellishing.

2. Cut away the damaged center of the doily. Fold under the cut edge a scant 1/4", clipping the seam if necessary, and press. Position the doily at the center of the muslin, and pin it in place.

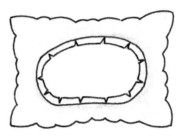

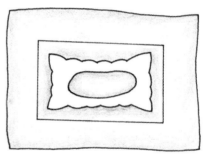

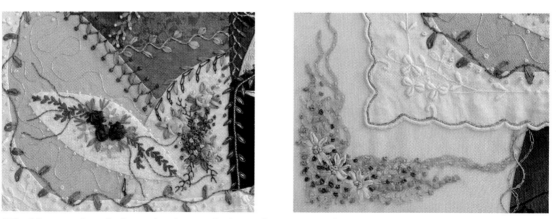

Silk ribbon motifs and other embroidery on the Framed Picture give the viewer much to look at.

3. Following instructions for the Antique Method (see page 8) of crazy patching, apply crazy patches inside and around the doily, tucking their edges under the doily, and having the patches go beyond the pencil line by at least 1/4". Lay the frame on occasionally to check that the outer raw edges will be concealed by the frame. When finished patching, machine- or hand-stitch around the outer edges to securely hold the patch edges in place. Place this stitching so it will not show after the piece is framed.

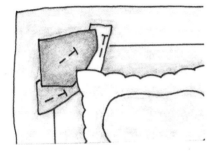

4. Embroider, using metallics couched by hand, and silk ribbon for some of the stitching along patch seams. Work silk ribbon embroideries on some of the patches. (I have couched Japan Gold #5 around the perimeter of the doily, and worked a meandering Outline stitch and silk ribbon Lazy Daisy stitch leaves around the cut-away edge.)

5. Place the piece face down on a terry cloth towel and press lightly without steam.

The remaining instructions are for framing the finished piece. You may prefer instead to take the needlework piece and frame to a framer to have it done professionally.

6. With the crazy quilt piece lying face down, place the foamcore onto it. Fold two opposite sides of the muslin onto the foamcore and pin. Thread a hand-sewing needle with size 50 or YLI Select cotton sewing thread, knot it, and begin lacing at one end, working toward the other end. Each time the thread runs out, snug up the laces and then fasten off. Begin a new thread and continue. The longer the thread, the less fastening off is done. Turn the piece over and lay the frame on to see that the crazy patching is properly centered. If not, carefully adjust the muslin.

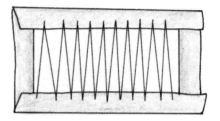

7. Repeat step 6 to lace the remaining two sides, keeping the piece properly centered.

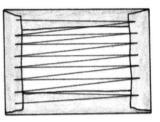

8. Secure the piece into the frame using brads or glass points. Cover the back of the piece with brown paper lightly glued to the back of the frame. No glass is used on the model shown. If you prefer to have glass over the needlework, have the picture matted using 2-3 mats so none of the fibers touch the glass.

Book Covers

Garden Notebook Cover

The Garden Notebook is a handy companion for making to-do lists and taking notes on-site.

Keep your gardening notes in order with a notebook for collecting thoughts and ideas, plans, seed lists, to-do lists, and maintenance schedules. Your garden plans or journal will be handy when kept in a spiral notebook with its special Confetti-pieced Garden Notebook Cover. The notebook can be carried into the garden and used on-site.

The Confetti-pieced Garden Notebook Cover is custom fitted to any ordinary spiral notebook. The notebook used here is 6-1/2" wide by 9-1/2" long with rounded corners. Choose a notebook in the size of your preference with square or rounded corners. A spiral-bound artist's sketchbook may be used instead if you prefer unlined paper.

A handy front pocket keeps pen and pencil, and the flaps provide places to slip newspaper and magazine clippings for handy reference.

Making a Pattern

1. Begin with a piece of paper that is larger than the notebook when it is laid open. You may need to tape sheets of paper together. Trace the back cover of the spiral notebook as shown in the diagram.

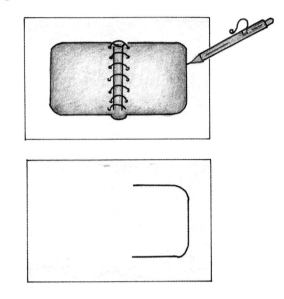

1.a. With the notebook closed, measure from the outer edge of the front cover, around to the outer edge of the back cover. Use this measurement to locate the position of the front cover on the paper. Make a pencil mark. Continue the lines

Materials

Spiral notebook, your desired size
Tape measure, ruler, pencil, plain paper
1/3 yard lengths of 6 different plain and printed quilting cotton fabrics
One 6-1/4" cut of the stacked fabrics is sufficient for a small notebook cover. Use two cuts for a larger cover (see Confetti Piecing, page 15)
Extra 1/4 yard of one of the prints for welting and ties
100-percent cotton sewing thread in a color to blend with the fabrics, and to match the lining fabric

To determine yardage for the following, lay the notebook open and purchase a sufficient amount:
    Firmly woven cotton fabric for lining
    Double-faced cotton flannel fabric for interlining
    3/16" cotton filler cord for welting-measure completely around the outer edge of the notebook

1/2" seam allowance is used throughout. Prewash fabrics.

of the drawing to complete the pattern. If the notebook has rounded corners, lay the book in place on the pattern and trace around its corners.

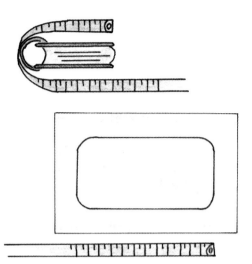

2. With the ruler, add 5/8" to the outer edges of the drawing. Of this, 1/8" is for "ease" to allow the notebook enough space to slide in and out of the cover, with the remaining 1/2" for the seam allowance.

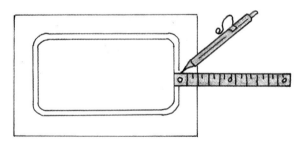

2.a. Draw straight lines where the spiral meets the cardboard of the notebook. This will be used for the flap and pocket patterns. If you wish to preserve the cover

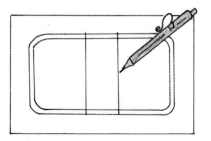

pattern intact, trace off the flap section onto separate paper.

Note: If making the cover for the first time, following the instructions using scrap fabric is recommended.

Assembling the Notebook Cover

1. Following instructions for Confetti Piecing on page 15, make a piece of Confetti the size of the pattern. Cut out the completed pattern, and use it to cut one each of Confetti, double-faced flannel, and lining fabric.

2. Using the flap pattern, cut 4 pieces of lining fabric. Two of these will be used to make pockets; see next step.

3. Choose a pen or pencil to be used with the notebook. Place this on a flap piece so the writing tip will be above the lower seam allowance. Mark on the flap with a pin where the top of the clip will rest. Fold the piece evenly 1/2" above this mark, and cut on the fold line. Cut out a second pocket for the remaining flap.

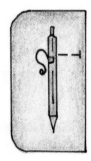

4. Turn the upper edge of each pocket 1/4" to the back twice, and press. Top-

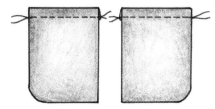

stitch each. Place one pocket on each of the flap pieces, and pin.

4.a. Turn under the inner edge of each flap/pocket piece 1/2" to the back twice, and press. Topstitch each. Sew lines to keep pencils and pens separated.

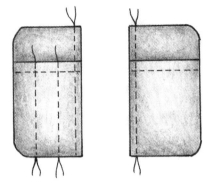

4.b. Place and pin the flaps wrong sides down on the right side of the lining. Set aside.

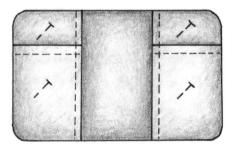

5. To make ties, cut 4 pieces of the extra 1/4 yard piece of fabric, each 1-3/4" by 7-1/4". Place 2 pieces with right sides together and sew around three sides. Trim, turn, press. Repeat for the remaining tie. Place raw edges of ties to the right side of the Confetti cover, centering them. Pin and baste.

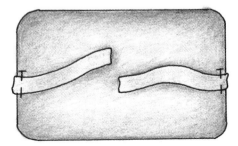

6. Make the length needed of 1-1/2" wide bias out of the extra 1/4 yard piece of fabric (see Bias Binding instructions on page 139), and make welting using the cotton filler cord, following instructions on page 142. Pin the welting to the right side of the cover matching the seamlines and overlapping the ends. Baste, then clip corners.

7. With right sides together, place the lining and the cover together. Add interlining over that, and pin. Sew around, leaving an opening to turn. Trim seams, turn, press. Slipstitch the opening closed.

Photo Log Cover

This Photo Log contains documentation of my antique roses and other perennials.

Materials

Binder-type photo book of desired size
Other materials same as for the Garden Notebook Cover

1/2" seam allowances are used throughout. Prewash fabrics.

There are many reasons to keep a garden photo log. Use a log to capture the fleeting beauty of once-flowering roses, for wintertime appreciation of the flowers you've cultivated, as an aid in landscape planning, to inspire needlework design ideas, and to show the results of your hard work to others. If you are beginning a landscaping project, consider filling a "photo diary" with before and after pictures. Organize them into a binder-style photo book with a Confetti-pieced Photo Log Cover to match the Garden Notebook.

The Photo Log Cover is very similar to the Notebook cover, except that it is made to fit a ring binder instead of a spiral notebook. Any style or size of ring binder may be used.

1. Tape sheets of paper together if necessary. Lay the binder (photo book) open on the paper and trace around accurately. With the ruler, add an additional 5/8" all around. Of this, 1/8" is for "ease," and the remaining 1/2" is for the seam allowance.

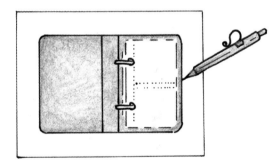

2. Draw a straight line where the photo book cover bends when it closes. This section will be used for the flap and pocket patterns. If you wish to preserve the cover pattern intact, trace off the flap section onto separate paper.

Note: If making the cover for the first time, following the instructions using scrap fabric is recommended.

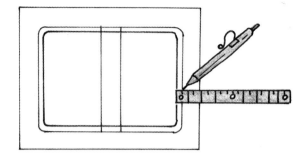

3. Following instructions for Confetti Piecing on page 15, make a piece of Confetti the size of the pattern. Cut out the completed pattern, and use it to cut one each of Confetti, double-faced flannel, and lining fabric.

4. If pockets are desired, follow instructions 2-4 of the Garden Notebook Cover. The following instructions are for making flaps without pockets.

4.a. Using the flap pattern, cut 2 pieces of lining fabric. Turn under the inner edge of each flap piece 1/2" to the back twice, and press. Topstitch each.

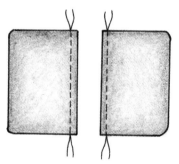

4.b. Place the flaps wrong sides down on the right side of the lining. Set aside.

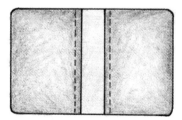

To finish the cover, follow steps 5-7 of the Garden Notebook Cover.

Antique Method Scrapbook Cover

It is easy to make a book cover using the Antique Method of crazy patching.

Materials

3" ring binder, or desired size
Tape measure, ruler, pencil, plain paper, tissue paper
Scraps of fabrics for patches, cotton types or other washable fabrics, 5-6 solids and one
    soft print in your choice of colors
Embellishments such as ribbons, laces, braids, and cording including two Venice trims
    (5-1/2" x 3") to decorate the oval area
Size 8 pearl cotton threads for embroidery, 8 - 10 colors of your choice
1/4 yard of a quilting cotton fabric for welting and ties, a soft print
Sewing thread to match the welting and lining fabrics

To determine yardage for the following, lay the binder open and purchase a sufficient
    amount:
100-percent cotton muslin
Firmly woven cotton fabric for lining
Double-faced cotton flannel fabric for interlining
3/16" cotton filler cord, a length to go around the outer edge of the cover

1/2" seam allowance is used throughout. Prewash fabrics.

It is easy to make a hand-patched, embroidered, and embellished cover for a scrapbook or memories album by following the instructions for the Photo Log Cover. Decorate the cover with laces as the one shown here, or collect things to sew on. You can add charms, buttons, clothing labels, beads, and other things. Use mementos such as small award pins and ribbons, photos transferred onto fabric (ask for this service at your local photocopier), and other items that can be sewn on.

For pages, use any that work for what you are doing with the scrapbook. Some of the pages can be for photos, others for drawings, and still others for gluing things onto. Use a hole punch to fit sheets of paper to the three rings of the binder. Check with an arts and crafts supply shop for additional scrapbooking materials.

Using the Tissue Paper Transfer Method (page 141), hand-write a title for the scrapbook on the tissue paper. Choose one of the scrap fabrics,  and draw an oval (or the shape of your choice) onto the fabric. Center the title inside the drawn oval and baste the tissue

paper in place. Embroider the title in Outline or other stitch. Cut out the title in an oval or the shape of your choice allowing 1/4" for a seam allowance. Press the allowance under.

Follow instructions for the Photo Log Cover with the following exception: for step 3, do not make the Confetti crazy quilt fabric. Instead, cut out the completed pattern and use it to cut one each of muslin, double-faced flannel, and lining fabric. Following instructions for the Antique Method on page 8, apply patches to the muslin, using the embroidered title at the center of the front of the cover (lay the piece onto the binder to check placement). Outline the title oval using cording, lace, or other trim. Apply any desired embellishments, and work embroidery along the patch seams. Press.

Continue with step 4 of the Photo Log Cover, substituting the patched muslin for the Confetti.

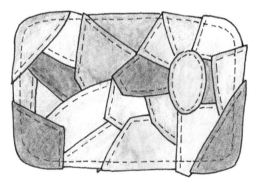

The scrapbook is all ready for Rachel to insert her art works, photos, and other mementos.

Chapter 5

Cradle Capers

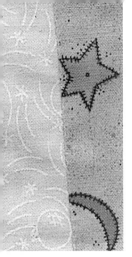

Strip Patching and Appliqué

A simple appliquéd star-shape becomes a theme for a baby's ensemble. Made in soft shades to give it an aged look, this set appears as if it already has been lovingly handed on to the newest generation. The complete ensemble makes an ideal new-baby gift, although one or two pieces of it would likely be as welcome. Quality made pieces are soon outgrown, but live on as they can be put aside to keep for the next generation, or simply handed on in a large family.

This set is designed for the tiniest of tots—what a perfect gift set for a baby shower or the newborn! The Cradle Capers Crib Quilt and the Jacket can also be made in larger sizes. Use any jacket pattern that is made of simple shapes and follow the instructions using sufficient cuts of the Confetti fabrics. Make the quilt larger by increasing the number of blocks used, adding to the amounts of fabrics as necessary and making the border to fit.

Projects:

Cradle Capers Crib Quilt

Star Doll Toys

Baby's Jacket

Star Bib

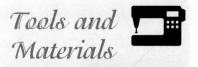

Tools and Materials

Muslin fabric for foundation

Fabrics for patches (cotton quilting fabrics are used for Confetti projects)

100-percent cotton sewing thread to blend with the fabrics

Fabric shears, iron

Strip Patching

Strip Patching is a quick and easy method of applying patches of fabric to a narrow piece of foundation by machine. Small pieces of fabric are sewn one onto the next, skewing each slightly for an unevenness that is characteristic of crazy quilting. Here the technique is used to make a border for a crib-size quilt. (The topic of Strip Patching is treated in greater depth in my book, *Crazy Quilts by Machine*, Krause, 2000.)

1. Begin with a strip of muslin foundation fabric, and with patch fabrics cut slightly wider than the foundation. Place one patch at the beginning of the foundation. The easiest way to proceed is to sew on a patch fabric without first cutting it to size. After the seam is sewn and pressed, trim away any excess, leaving the patch the size you want it to be. Try to make each patch slightly different in size and shape.

2. Place a second patch with right sides together onto the first and sew a 1/4" seam.

3. Open out the patch, and press. As each patch is added, trim away any excess fabric from the seam allowance of the previous patch. Do not cut the foundation.

4. Place a third patch onto the second and sew the seam. Open out the patch and press.

Continue until the foundation is covered. Trim the patches even with sides of the foundation.

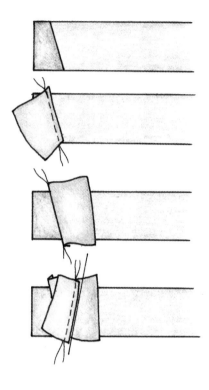

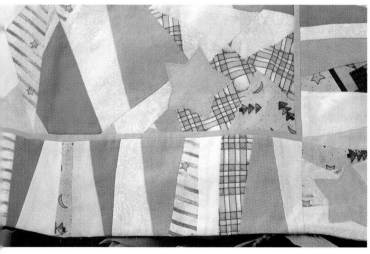

The Cradle Capers quilt border is strip patched.

Machine Appliqué

Machine Appliqué is an easy way to apply a simple fabric shape onto a background fabric.

One of the print fabrics selected for the Cradle Capers quilt suggested the star-shape that is used in three of the projects. The idea to draft the star larger to make a doll toy was no more than a moment's inspiration. You may like to design an appliqué in a shape of your choosing. Consider simplified shapes such as a moon, a house, or car.

1. Trace and cut out the Star Appliqué Pattern (see page 88), or the pattern of your choice. Out of the appliqué fabric, cut out the shape adding a 1/4" to 1/8" seam allowance.

2. Machine sew the appliqué to the background fabric along the seam line.

3. With a sharp scissors, trim the seam allowance as near to the stitching as possible.

4. Experimenting on scrap fabric, set the machine to a zigzag width that will cover both the seam and the edge of the fabric, and a short stitch length so that the stitches fall directly next to each other. Zigzag completely around the appliqué, then set the machine to zero stitch length and width and sew several stitches to fasten off. Remove the piece from the machine, and trim the ends close to the stitching.

Background fabric
Appliqué fabric
Small sharp scissors, or appliqué scissors
Sewing machine that does zigzag stitching
100-percent cotton sewing thread
Tracing paper, pencil, scissors

Look around you for appliqué motif ideas. The head of this rocking horse, for instance, would make a charming motif and is a simple enough shape.

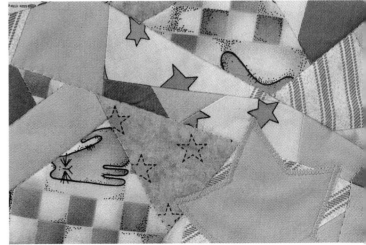

Machine-sewn appliqués are simple to do.

Cradle Capers Crib Quilt

Finished size: 30" x 44". The quilt is made of four blocks each 13" by 20", and a 4-1/2" wide border.

The Cradle Capers Crib Quilt shown draped over a wooden rocking horse.

Materials

1/3 yard lengths of 8 different quilting cotton fabrics including child-like prints in soft shades of off-white, beige, green and blue (see Confetti Piecing, page 15)
100-percent cotton sewing thread in a color to blend with the quilting fabrics, and golden yellow for appliqué
1-1/2 yards of 100-percent cotton muslin for foundations
30" x 44" piece of medium-weight 100-percent cotton fabric for backing, any coordinating color
30" x 44" piece of cotton batting
YLI Quilting or Select thread, Ecru

1/4" seam allowances are used throughout

Cutting: cut the muslin into four 5" squares, two borders each 5" x 25-1/2", two borders each 5" x 39-1/2", and one piece 25-1/2" x 39-1/2" for the quilt foundation.

Easy appliqué and strip patching are used in conjunction with Confetti crazy piecing for this charming baby's quilt. Colors chosen for this project are mellow, antique shades of off-whites, beige, green, and blue to give the quilt a soft, "country" look. The prints used include striped, plaid, and child-like star and moon prints. The golden yellow color is "borrowed" from the prints, and used in both the flange and the appliquéd stars.

1. After taking four cuts (6-1/4" x 12") of the 1/3 yard lengths of quilting cottons, set aside the remaining fabric to be used for the strip-patched border.

2. With the four cuts of quilting cotton fabrics, out of each make a 13" x 20" block following instructions for the Confetti Method (see page 15). Out of the cut-offs from these blocks, make four pieces each 5" square for the corner blocks. Line each corner block with a 5" square of muslin.

3. Sew the blocks together with 1/4" seams to make one piece 25-1/2" x 39-1/2". Press the seams to one side. Place the 25-1/2" x 39-1/2" muslin foundation onto the back 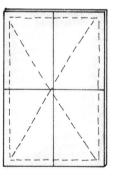 of the quilt top. Baste around, then baste across the quilt top to prevent shifting.

4. Out of the golden yellow, cut four flange pieces, each 1" wide. Cut two 25-1/2" long, and two 39-1/2" long. Press the strips in half lengthwise with wrong sides together. Matching raw edges, place and pin the two 39-1/2" strips along the sides of the quilt, and the 25-1/2" strips at the top and bottom. Baste.

5. Follow instructions for Machine Appliqué on page 85 to appliqué one star to each corner block, and eight stars evenly distributed over the quilt top.

6. Strip Patch the four muslin border pieces, according to instructions on page 84.

7. Sew the longer pieces to the sides of the quilt. Sew a corner block to each end of the shorter pieces, then sew them to the ends of the quilt. Press the seams toward the borders, and the flange toward the quilt top.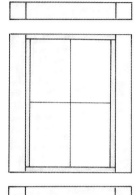

The borders and flanges of the crib quilt.

8. Assemble the layers of the quilt with wrong sides together: backing, batting, and quilt top. Baste throughout the quilt with thread or safety pins; see page 139. Quilt the layers by 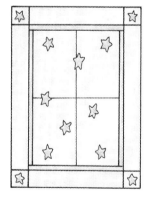 stitching in the ditch (page 140) in enough places to securely hold the layers. Use YLI Select or quilting thread.

9. Finish the outer edge of the quilt by turning in the edges and slipstitching (see page 141).

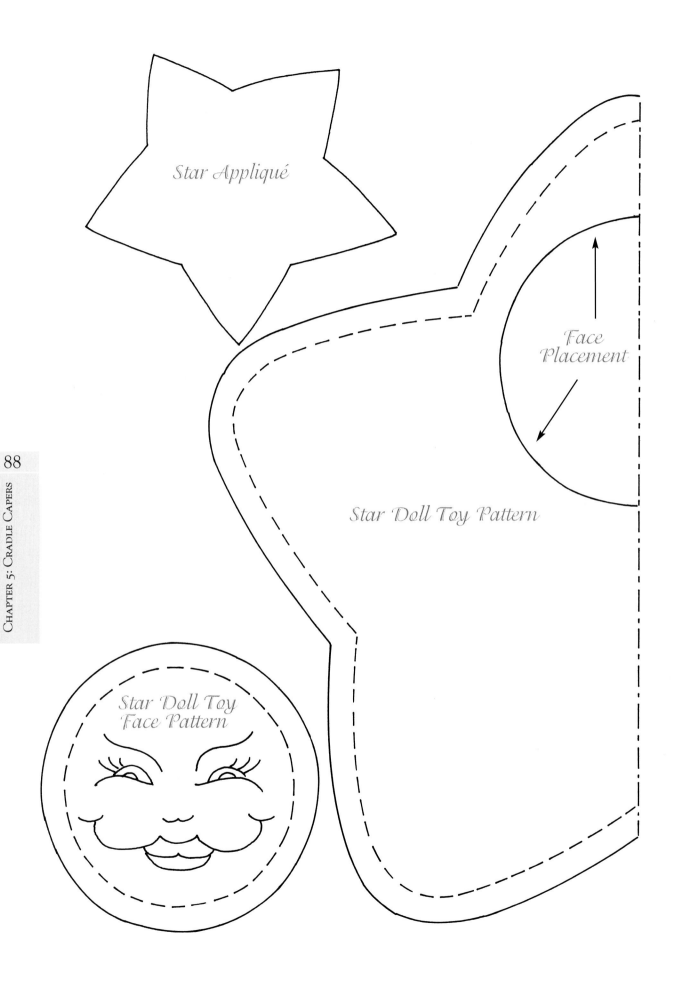

Star Appliqué

Face
Placement

Star Doll Toy Pattern

Star Doll Toy
Face Pattern

Star Doll Toys

Make this doll in sets of three to capture the different angle of the faces.

Materials

Pencil, tracing paper, scissors
1 - 2 cuts (each 4-3/4" x 9") of:
   1/4 yard lengths of 8 different quilting cotton fabrics including child-like prints in
   soft shades of off-white, beige, green and blue (see Confetti Piecing, page 15)
100-percent cotton sewing thread in a color to blend with the quilting fabrics, and
   golden yellow for appliqué
1/4 yard of 100-percent cotton muslin
1/4 yard of medium-weight 100-percent cotton fabric for backing, any coordinating color
Permanent fabric pen, fine or medium point, black
Stuffing

Make three of these charming toys to show the different angles of the faces. These happy fellows are simple to make. Materials as given here are sufficient for three dolls.

1. Work Confetti Piecing following instructions on page 15, making enough for 3 doll toys.

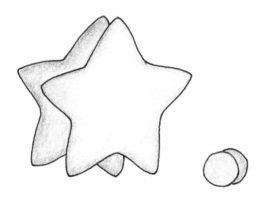

2. Trace and cut out the Star Doll pattern, and the face pattern. For each doll, cut one each of Confetti, muslin, and backing fabric using the Star Doll pattern, and one each of yellow fabric and muslin using the face pattern.

3. To make the face, transfer the facial features as follows: Trace the facial lines, then use a dark pen to go over them. Tape the pattern to a window. Place the yellow face piece over the pattern, and trace the features in pencil. Remove from the window and trace over the lines using the permanent pen. Make one for each doll.

Place the faces on an ironing board and lay a press cloth over them. Heat-set the ink by placing an iron set on wool (no steam) on each of the faces for at least 20 seconds. Place a piece of muslin on the back of each of the yellow pieces.

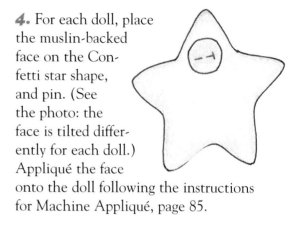

4. For each doll, place the muslin-backed face on the Confetti star shape, and pin. (See the photo: the face is tilted differently for each doll.) Appliqué the face onto the doll following the instructions for Machine Appliqué, page 85.

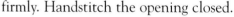

5. Place the backing fabric right sides together with the Confetti star piece; pin, and sew around leaving an opening to turn the doll. Trim seams, clipping to the inner corners. Turn, press. Stuff firmly. Handstitch the opening closed.

The bodice of this doll's dress was crazy patched using the Antique Method. This was easily done by cutting the bodice pattern pieces (front and back) out of muslin. The muslin was patched and embroidered, and then the garment was sewn according to the pattern instructions.

Baby's Jacket

Size: any baby or toddler pattern size. Increase the number of cuts of Confetti fabrics for larger sizes, as needed. The size shown here is for a baby of 6 months.

Baby's jacket is a simple shape and easy to make.

Materials

Commercial pattern for a simple, unlined baby's jacket

3 cuts (each 4-3/4" x 9") of the 1/4 yard lengths of the 8 different quilting cotton fabrics as used for the Star Doll Toys

100-percent cotton sewing thread in a color to blend with the quilting fabrics, and golden yellow for appliqué and binding

1/2 yard of medium-weight 100-percent cotton fabric for bias binding and applique, golden yellow

Medium-weight 100-percent cotton fabric for lining, same yardage as for the jacket, any coordinating color

Buttons, snaps, or hook and loop fastener closures, your choice or as called for by the pattern

This jacket can be made in any baby, toddler, or child size. Select a commercial pattern for an unlined baby's jacket made of plain, simple shapes. The jacket shown here is made with a lining that is cut the same as the jacket pieces. No batting is used, and buttons are optional. You could make ties, or use small pieces of hook and loop fastener instead.

1. Using the golden yellow fabric, make 2 yards of 1-1/4" wide bias for binding (see Bias Binding instructions, page 139).

2. With the three cuts of the Confetti fabrics, work Confetti Piecing following instructions on page 15. (Additional cuts may be needed for larger sizes.) Out of the Confetti, cut two jacket fronts, one back, and two sleeves. Cut the same pieces out of the lining fabric. Machine appliqué a star shape to one jacket front, placing as shown on the diagram. See Machine Appliqué instructions, page 85.

3. With right sides together, sew the jacket fronts to the jacket back at the shoulders. Press the seams to one side. Sew on the sleeves. Sew the arm and side seams.

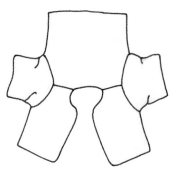

4. Sew the lining same as in step 3.

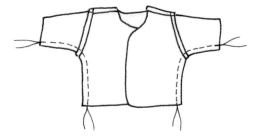

5. Trim away the seam allowances from the neck, sleeve ends, and bottom edges of both the jacket and the lining.

6. Place the lining inside the jacket with wrong sides together. Pin, matching seams and raw edges.

7. Follow instructions for Applying Bias Edging using the Sew 'n Slipstitch Method on page 141 to apply bias binding to all raw edges. Add buttons, snaps, or hook and loop fastener closures.

Optional: the layers of the jacket can be tied with the ties to the inside, page 142, or machine-quilted, page 140. For quilting, use ecru quilting thread, and the quilting pattern of your choice, or stitch in the ditch (page 140).

 Star Bib

Teddy seems pleased with his bib.

Materials

1-2 cuts (each 4-3/4" x 9") of the 1/4 yard lengths of 8 different quilting
  cotton fabrics as used for the Star Doll Toys

100-percent cotton sewing thread in a color to blend with the quilting fabrics, and
  golden yellow for appliqué and binding

Paper, pencil, tracing paper

9" x 11" piece of cotton batting

9" x 11" piece of medium-weight 100-percent cotton fabric for backing, any coordinating color

1/2 yard of medium-weight 100-percent cotton fabric for bias binding and applique,
  golden yellow (same as used for the Baby' s Jacket)

YLI Quilting or Select thread, ecru

Make a bib to complete the ensemble. The method given below is for attaching the bias binding and ties in a way that the finished bib will be heirloom-quality and therefore suitable for gift-giving. In case you are making a bib for utilitarian purposes, you may substitute purchased double-fold bias binding instead. Sew it on where called for by encasing the edge of the bib in the bias tape, and topstitching by machine to join all layers.

1. Work Confetti Piecing following instructions on page 15.

2. To make a pattern, tape sheets of paper together if necessary to make a 9" x 11" rectangle.

3. Trace the pattern for the bib neck opening, and use it to cut the neck opening in the pattern. Round the four corners as desired. Cut one each of Confetti, batting, and backing.

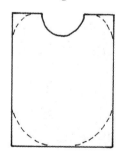

4. Cut one star out of the yellow fabric, and appliqué it onto the bib following Machine Appliqué instructions on page 85.

5. Assemble the layers. Quilt by stitching in the ditch (see page 140) using Quilting or Select thread.

6. Prepare two lengths of bias binding, 1-1/4" wide by 30" long (Bias Binding instructions, page 139). Following Applying Bias Edging using the Sew 'n Slipstitch Method instructions on page 141, machine sew and slipstitch one of the lengths around the outer edge of the bib. Sew the center of the second length to the neck edge. To finish, fold in the bias 1/4" at each long edge, fold in half lengthwise, and slipstitch. Fold in the ends and finish neatly.

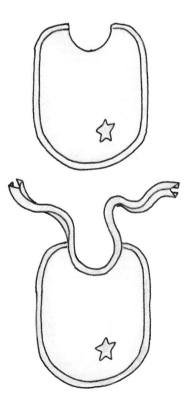

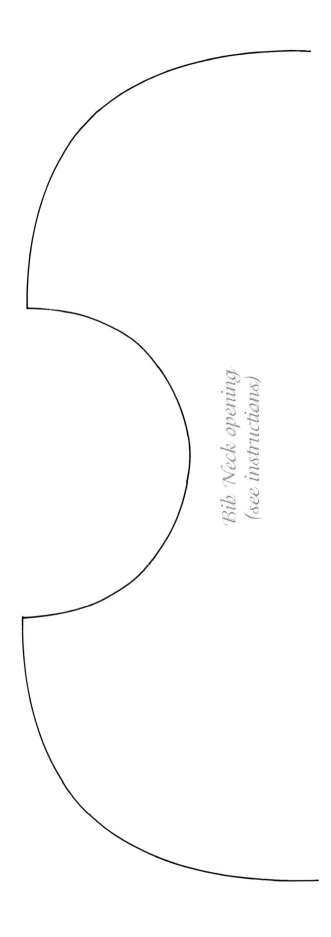

*Bib Neck opening
(see instructions)*

Chapter 6

For the Gents

Gift ideas for the guys: give them something they can use and enjoy.

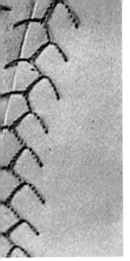

Wool Embroidery

Here are three practical gifts for men. He'll enjoy wearing a silk tie especially made for him, warming up under his lap robe on a cool evening, and lounging in his bathrobe with its Confetti quilted collar. Make the tie extra special by hand-dying the silk patch fabrics.

Wool embroidery is easy to learn using wool threads, but the stitches may also be done using silk, rayon, or cotton threads. The pinecone design given here makes use of only two embroidery stitches: the Bullion Stitch and Couching.

Projects:

Piney Woods Lap Robe

Silk Tie

Bathrobe Collar

Materials

Chenille needles, assorted sizes
Persian wool threads, 3 shades of
   brown, 2 of green
Embroidery hoop
Embroidery Scissors

Tools and materials for wool embroidery are minimal.

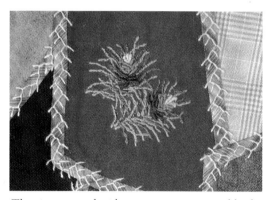

The pinecone embroidery is as pretty on a red background as on a light color.

Flowers such as these lilacs can be replicated dimensionally in wool using French Knots.

Wool Embroidery

Wool embroidery makes use of many stitches including dimensional ones and couching. Similar to Silk-Ribbon embroidery, stitches are used to form leaves, flower petals and other objects. Here, Bullion stitches simulate actual pine cones, mimicking their forms and suggesting the layers of the wood they are formed out of, while pine needles are suggested by long, couched stitches.

The Bullion Stitch is dimensional, lying above the fabric upon which it is made. Although it may appear complicated, it is actually quite easy to do, especially with wool threads. Once you learn how, try the stitch in silk, cotton, or rayon threads.

Most often I use one strand of the Persian wool, but you may also use two or three strands for making the Bullion stitch, depending on how large you want the finished stitch to be. Experiment to find your preference, using a needle that fits the number of strands. For Couching the pine needles, use one strand.

When you are embroidering through both wool and foundation fabrics, an embroidery hoop is not always needed, and some hoops will not accommodate the thickness. Try using a hoop if you find that your stitches are causing the fabric to bunch.

Begin by making several tiny stitches close together on the back of the work to secure the thread. Bring the needle up through the fabric. Make the Bullion stitch according to instructions on page 11.

The Bullion stitch can be shaped in a slight curve. Add a stitch over the Bullion to hold the curve in place.

Couching is done by taking a long stitch, then bringing the needle up near one end of the stitch. Make tiny tacking stitches along the long couched stitch, with the same thread, shaping it as desired. See the instructions on page 12. I couched a soft curve into the pine needles; you can make them straight or curved.

You can trace the embroidery pattern given here, using the Tissue Paper Transfer Method (page 141) to transfer the design, or follow the sequence of stitching and freehand it. It is easiest to work the embroidery on the patches after they have been added to the foundation fabric, the extra layer providing a stabilizer and a place to work the beginnings and ends of threads into.

The Couched pine needles will be easiest to add freehand. Fill in with the pine needles until the design appears complete.

Examples of wool embroidery worked on the Horses and Roses wool quilt (this quilt is featured in my book The Magic of Crazy Quilting)*.*

Piney Woods Lap Robe

Size: 36" square.

The lap quilt displayed in a forest setting.

Materials

36" square muslin fabric for foundation

Scraps of wool fabrics in a mix of types including suitings, coatings, and others in browns, greys, green, red, and cream

YLI Basting & Bobbin thread

1 yard of 100-percent cotton quilting fabric in a blending print

100-percent cotton sewing thread to blend with the quilting fabric

36" square cotton fabric for backing, any coordinating color

*Persian wool threads in three shades of brown and one of green

Chenille needle for embroidery

Optional: bias tape maker

*Paternayan Persian colors used are the browns: 432, 430, and 436, and the greens 600 and 602.

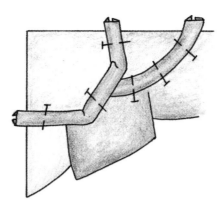

The patching method used for this lap robe is a variation of the Antique Method. Instead of turning the edges of the patches under, they are simply overlapped and then covered with bias binding. This is a way of avoiding the added bulk of a turned-under edge, and makes a neat finish for the patches. Make your own bias using a soft print of a quilting cotton fabric.

Pinecones and pine needles are lavishly embroidered in wool using Bullion Stitch and Couching.

1. Place patches onto the muslin foundation following instructions for the Antique Method on page 8, but have the patches over- and under-lap only about 1/4" to 1/2". Baste the patches placing the basting stitches about 3/4" in from the edges of the patches. Do not turn the edges under.

2. Cut bias strips 1" wide following instructions for Bias Binding, page 139. Make single-fold bias following instructions on page 140. With an iron, and by hand or using a bias tape maker, press under the long edges 1/4".

3. As you make the binding, cut pieces of it and lay in place as follows. Place a piece of bias so that it covers the raw edge of a patch, and pin. Tuck the ends under the edges of adjoining patches. Continue to make and place the bias pieces until all overlapped patch edges are covered.

4. The next can be done by hand or by machine. By hand (recommended for an heirloom finish): work slipstitching along both edges of each bias piece. By machine (use where durability is more important than heirloom quality), topstitch along both edges of each bias piece. Keep looking for the next-most-underlapped patch, sew the bias, and continue.

5. Work pinecone embroideries on several of the quilt's patches following instructions on page 99.

6. Out of the cotton quilting fabric, cut bias strips 1-1/4" wide (see Bias Binding instructions page 139) and sew them together to make two lengths each 36" long. Follow instructions for Applying Bias Edging using the Sew 'n Slipstitch Method on page 140 to apply one to each side of the quilt. Make two additional lengths of bias each 37" long. Sew one to the top, and the other to the bottom of the quilt, clean finishing the short ends.

Silk Tie

The silk ties displayed in an antique trunk.

Materials

An old tie (or a commercial pattern)

1-1/3 yards of 100-percent cotton batiste fabric for foundation

Lightweight silk fabric scraps or small pieces, such as habotai, jacquard, and others, solid colors of your choice, about 6 colors per tie

2 to 3 spools of Soie Gobelin, a contrasting color of your choice, or other twisted silk-thread

Acetate lining fabric for the tips of the tie, small piece

Piece of wool for lining the length of the tie (obtained from the old tie)

100-percent cotton sewing thread to blend with the tie colors

Silk Tie

To make this project, a commercial pattern may be used, or take apart an old tie that is no longer wanted. Find one amongst your household possessions, or purchase one inexpensively at a used clothing outlet. Taking apart an old tie is preferable for three reasons. First, you can observe how a tie is put together. Secondly, the long, narrow lining inside is reusable. And, lastly, the tie fabric can be washed, pressed and used in a crazy quilting project. If there is a designer's name label I also put that aside to later sew onto a crazy quilt as a small decoration.

Because of the practicality of using an old tie, the instructions below assume this is being done. If you prefer to use a commercial pattern instead, follow its instructions with the exception of purchasing a fabric for the tie. Instead, substitute the foundation and patch fabrics as called for below.

The colors used in the light-colored tie are hand-dyed shades of blue, pink, greens, purple, and brown. The tie is embroidered in medium brown Soie Gobelin thread. The darker tie consists of deep shades of red, blue, purple, and is embroidered in light-gray thread.

1. Carefully take the old tie apart. Set aside the long piece of wool lining for use later. The two end linings at the tips of the tie can remain in 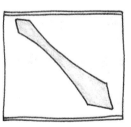 place; however, be sure to add seam allowances to your foundation in these areas. Press the tie fabric.

2. Lay the old tie fabric onto the foundation diagonally in order to cut the foundation on the bias. Pin. Cut out the foun-

Dyeing Silks

The pastel tie shown here consists of white and light-colored silks that were hand-dyed. Dyeing silks in small amounts is very easy. Use "Colorhue" dyes from Things Japanese, distilled water, and a small container such as a plastic dish (do not reuse for eating) for each color. Using one eyedropper per dye, add a few drops of a color to about 1/2 cup of distilled water. Add dye and mix colors until you have a color you want. Put in a small piece of fabric, perhaps about 9" square, and leave it scrunched in the dye for a few minutes. This will achieve a mottled effect. For a more even effect, stir the fabric while it is in the solution. Remove the silk with a tweezers, and place it on a paper towel. When finished dyeing, gently wash the dyed silks in cool water with a tiny amount of gentle soap added (I use natural shampoo). Roll the rinsed silks in a towel, remove from the towel and allow to dry. Press. Instructions for mixing dye colors appear in The Magic of Crazy Quilting.

The soft colors of this tie are produced by hand dyeing silk fabrics.

dation the same as the old tie fabric, adding seam allowances at the tips if you have not removed the tip linings. Only a small amount of the 1-1/3 yards of batiste fabric is actually being used. Retain the cut-offs for other projects. Once the foundation is cut, handle it carefully—being bias cut it is prone to stretching.

Note: see "Using Silks," chapter 8, page 135.

3. Using the Antique Method of patching, patch the entire foundation with the silk fabrics. Baste the patches in place, and baste around the outer edges of the tie. Press lightly on the wrong side using a dry iron and with the tie lying on a terry cloth towel. Whenever the tie-in-progress should require pressing, use this method.

4. Embroider along the patch seams using Soie Gobelin thread and the stitch or stitches of your choice.

5. Assemble the tie. The following is what I learned from taking a tie apart. First, line the tips. Cut the acetate lining fabric the same as the tips at both ends of the tie and about 3" long (use the patched tie as a pattern). Trim away 1/8" from the two edges of the tip of the lining. Press these edges under 1/2". Press the sides under beginning with 1/2" at the lower end and tapering to nothing.

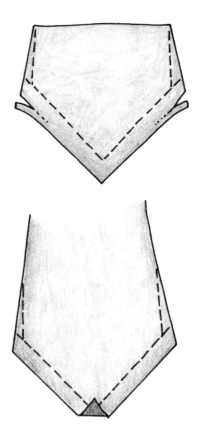

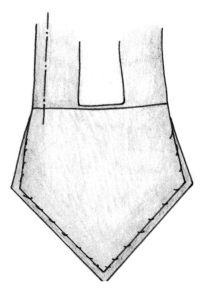

6. Press the tips of the tie the same except do not trim. Miter the tips as shown in the diagram. Place the linings on the wrong side of the tie leaving a 1/8" gap at the tip edges. Pin, then slipstitch the lining in place (in the old tie, the lining was machine-sewn, but it is much easier to slipstitch it by hand in order to replicate its placement).

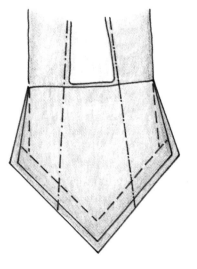

7. Press under 1/2" on one long edge of the tie. Fold the tie in thirds lengthwise along the same fold lines as the old tie. Overlap the pressed edge 1/2" onto the raw edge. Pin. Loosely slipstitch along the tie center using long stitches.

8. Finally, very lightly press the tie having it face down on a terry towel, with a dry iron. Do not allow creases to form at the edges.

The best way to finish a tie is to carefully observe a purchased one, then apply your findings to the one you are making.

This Computer Equipment Dust Cover is made the same way as the toaster cover on page 65.
This cover is made to fit a laser printer. Whenever you are not sure about getting something to fit properly, always make a sample in scrap fabric. Make adjustments to the sample until the fit is as you intended. Then, take the sample apart and use it as a pattern for Confetti piecing or the muslin for the Antique method.

Bathrobe with Quilted Collar

Make this bathrobe according to a commercial pattern, but substitute a handsome confetti-pieced and quilted collar.

Materials

Commercial pattern for a shawl-collared bathrobe in the size needed

Fabric yardage as called for by the pattern

1/4 yard each of 8 different quilting cotton fabrics in light to medium shades of blue or the color of your choice (see Confetti Piecing instructions, page 15)

100-percent cotton batiste fabric, sufficient amount to back the two collar facings (see facing pattern piece)

1/2 yard of cotton fabric for bias binding, any coordinating color

100-percent cotton sewing thread to blend with the fabrics

YLI Basting & Bobbin thread

*Quilting thread in the color of your choice

   *Quilting thread used here is YLI's Select thread in the bobbin, and YLI's Quilting Thread threaded into the machine. Dark blue was used to have the quilting lines match the robe fabric, contrasting with the Confetti fabrics.

A bathrobe is an easy shape to sew. The basic bathrobe requires little fitting, has no buttonholes or zipper, and no lengthy instructions. Choose a basic shawl-collar pattern. The part of the pattern that is quilted is the collar facing. Set aside this pattern piece, and cut the remaining pieces out of the fabric you've chosen for the robe. Sew the entire robe, except the collar facing. Follow instructions below to make and assemble the collar facing.

Choose heavy flannel, cotton chamois cloth, or other solid-color woven fabric for the robe.

1. Stack the eight cotton quilting fabrics evenly and make four cuts (each 4-3/4" x 9"). Follow instructions for Confetti Piecing on page 15, joining the pieces to make one long piece wide enough for cutting out two collar facings. Cut out the facings. Also cut two of batiste the same. Place one batiste on the back of each Confetti facing, and handle the two as one.

2. To assemble the facing to the robe, first sew the back neck seam of the facing (following instructions with the pattern). Press the seam open or to one side. The outer edge of the facing will be sewn to the robe. For the inner edge, use the 1/2 yard of cotton fabric and follow instructions for Applying Bias Edging using the Sew 'n Slipstitch Method on page 140. Then sew the collar to the robe according to the pattern instructions.

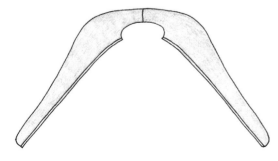

3. Lay the robe out with its fronts overlapped as it will be when worn, or place it on a hanger. Fold the collar along the

foldlines as it will be when worn. Put in some pins along the fold making sure the robe fabric is neatly aligned with the collar facing. Keeping the fold in place, hand baste along the foldline. Baste with your non-sewing hand inside the fold to keep the layers aligned. Keeping the fold, continue to add lines of basting between the foldline and the outer edge of the collar.

4. Lay the robe out flat and add lines of basting between the foldline and the inner edge of the collar. When finished, the collar should gently roll along the established fold line, and yet remain flat in other areas. Baste well enough that the collar can be machine quilted.

5. Machine quilt the collar as shown in the diagram, or use the quilting pattern of your choice.

Chapter 7

Family Events

Fancy quilted gift bags with their gold cord ties and silk ornaments spell a festive occasion.

Machine Couching

Presented here is a selection of ideas for family occasions and other useful things. Gift bags are an attractive way to bestow that special gift and can be re-used indefinitely, including a silk pouch that is a gift in itself. Also included are ornaments for holiday or everyday decor, and, not to forget the family pet, a jacket for the dog.

Projects:

Festive Gift Bags:

Confetti Gift Bag

Wine Gift Bag

Silk Jewelry Pouch

Silk Doll and Moon Ornaments

Dog's Jacket

These baskets of threads, yarns, and trims display some of the many materials that can be couched.

Machine Couching

Couching by machine is a form of machine embroidery, and consists of sewing a decorative material (thread, ribbon, braid, or other fiber) onto fabric. It is exclusive to some of the Confetti projects in this book, and is used to quilt the layers. Confetti pieced projects adapt readily to being quilted, since they are more akin to traditional quilting than is the Antique method of crazy patching. Couching on decorative materials enlivens the surface beyond what quilting with plain thread would do.

Experiment with machine thread/couching thread combinations for the many different effects that can be

Gift bags can be made and used for many different occasions.

achieved. Try rayon or silk thread in the machine, and the fiber or material of your choice for the couching fiber. I like the sparkle of the metallics, but you can also try rayon or silk ribbons, cotton, silk, and rayon embroidery threads that are too heavy to thread into the sewing machine, and various types of cordings, trims, and even knitting yarns: angora, mohair, and others. Experiment with different materials on scrap fabrics. (Save your experimental pieces to be used as patch fabrics for your next Antique Method project.)

Couching is easiest if begun at one end of the piece, and ended at the other. This way the trimmed thread ends will be sewn into a seam allowance or bias-bound, leaving no ends showing. Couch in zigzag, waving, or meandering lines. You can also work in straight lines, vertically and/or horizontally, or diagonally.

Couched materials used in the Confetti Pieced projects in this chapter include Kreinik's fine, medium, and very fine metallic braids, and 1/16" metallic ribbon.

Thread into the machine a thread that will contrast with or enhance the couching material. Use Kreinik's Cord, or a rayon or silk thread intended for machine sewing. I have found that cord is sufficiently sturdy to eliminate frequent breakage.

Begin by hand basting the layered piece that will be couched. There will usually be three layers: lining, a batting or batting substitute, and the Confetti layer. Stack and pin them as they will be when

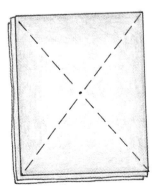

- Use a machine needle made for metallics
- Have size 50, 100-percent cotton sewing thread in the bobbin
- Use an embroidery foot, or the foot recommended in the machine's manual
- Set the machine tension toward the lower numbers (I use #4). This is to bring the couching thread to the back of the fabric so the bobbin thread will not be visible on the front
- Use a zigzag stitch that allows the needle to plunk down on either side of the couching material, without going into it
- Sew slowly

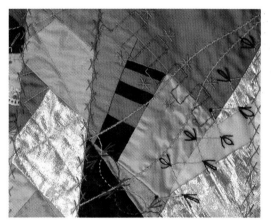

Machine couching can be placed across the patches of a crazy quilt as here on the Browns and Golds Strippie Quilt (this quilt is featured in my book, Crazy Quilts by Machine).

Interesting wood grains can suggest patterns for couching.

the project is finished. Use 100-percent cotton sewing thread, or YLI's Basting & Bobbin thread. Begin basting at the center and work to the outer edges, making diagonal lines. Then make lines going across and vertically.

Finish by hand-basting around the outer edge.

Begin couching the chosen material beginning at the edge of the quilted piece. Secure by backstitching within the seam allowance. With the couching material thus secured, lay the couching material in the desired pattern and begin zigzagging over it. End each line of couching at the lower end of the quilted piece, backstitching again to secure.

1. If using fibers of various sizes, sew on the boldest of the couching materials first, establishing the lines of your freeform design. Sew freeform lines that are curved, straight, or zigzag.

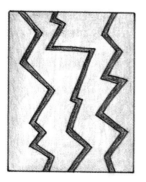

2. Add the next couching material, using a finer fiber than before, and couch so that spaces left earlier become filled in.

Be sure to work to the side edges so the sides will be as well-covered as the center of the piece.

3. Lastly, machine-straight-stitch lines (set the machine for the longest stitch length) to add additional lines of stitching as needed to fill in any unquilted areas.

Note: when pressing a piece that has materials couched onto it, observe the instructions of the manufacturer of that material. Often, a press cloth is required to avoid melting or damaging metallic and other fibers. Always use the lowest iron temperature possible, and avoid using steam.

Quilted Gift Bags

Gift bags can be reused many times and will always be appreciated.

Save paper (and trees) by making gift bags that will be treasured and re-used from one occasion to another. Choose fabric colors reminiscent of the occasion. For the Confetti and the Wine gift bags I have chosen faded reds and greens for the feeling of an old fashioned Christmas. For Hanukah choose blues and white, reds and white for Valentine's, whites and off-whites for a wedding, and so on. Brighten the fabrics by using metallic couching fibers, then dress up the bag with curly ribbons, tissue paper, and a fancy tag.

The jewelry pouch is designed to be made of the finest silk fabrics, trims, and fancy threads using the Antique Method of crazy patching. The size of the pouch can be adapted easily to accommodate small to larger pieces of jewelry. The pouch can then be kept by the recipient for storing the item.

Confetti Gift Bag

Size: 10" high, 8" wide, 4" deep.

*Couched metallic threads and gold cord are brilliant touches
against confetti piecing.*

Materials

1 - 2 cuts (each 4-3/4" x 9") of: 1/4 yard lengths of 8 different quilting cotton fabrics,
   your choice of colors (see Confetti Piecing, page 15)
100-percent cotton sewing thread to blend with the fabrics
13" x 24" piece of thin batting (poly or cotton)
13" x 24" piece of cotton fabric for lining, your choice of color
YLI Basting & Bobbin thread
Couching fibers and threads
1-1/4 yards of 3/16" rayon cording for handles

1/4" seam allowances

After making one bag following the sizes and directions below, you will see how to make a bag of any desired size. The bag begins with a simple rectangle of quilted fabric, then is sewn with two bottom corners, squaring its shape. The rectangle can be of any size: taller, wider, shorter, or narrower than the one shown here.

1. Following directions for Confetti Piecing, page 15, make one Confetti piece 13" x 24". Make a sandwich of lining fabric (right side down), batting, and the Confetti piece right side up. Baste and couch according to instructions for Machine Couching, page 110.

2. Fold the piece in half as shown in the diagram, with right sides together. Sew each side seam, then zigzag the seams.

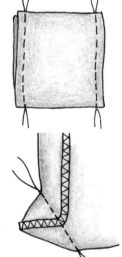

3. Pinch one of the bottom corners to form a triangular shape, centering the side seam. Measure to find where a seam sewn across will be 4" long, and sew across the triangle at that point. Trim the excess to leave a seam allowance of 1/4", and zigzag. Repeat for the other bottom corner.

4. Following instructions for Bias Binding on page 140, use one of the Confetti fabrics to make bias 1-1/4" wide by 25" long. Bind the upper edge of the bag according to instructions for applying bias edging using the Sew 'n Slipstitch Method on page 140. Fold the bag as if it were a brown paper bag, and press the folds.

5. Two inches from the top of the bag, and 1" in from the edge, push a pin through the layers at each side. Mark each layer individually where the pin has pierced by using an additional pin, or mark with chalk.

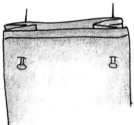

Sew a 3/4" buttonhole at each of the markings, making 8 buttonholes in all. String the cording through the buttonholes and tie a knot. Fluff the ends of the cording.

Greeting cards displaying your needle artworks are easy to make. Simply take photos of your work and lightly glue the photos to folded card stock. Use envelopes that are 6-1/2" wide by 4-3/4". Trim the folded card stock to fit inside the envelope, and trim the photo to fit the card. Use tiny drops of white glue to fasten the photo to the card and place under a heavy book until the glue is dry. The recipients will love seeing what you've been working on!

Wine Gift Bag

Size: approximately 14" long by 3-1/2" wide by 3-1/2" deep.

A Wine Gift Bag can be used to present a fancy bottle of wine, or to keep a chilled bottle cool.

Materials

Paper, pencil, tracing paper

2 cuts (each 4-3/4" x 9") of the 1/4 yards lengths of 8 different quilting cotton fabrics as used for the Confetti Gift Bag

100-percent cotton sewing thread to blend with the fabrics

1/4 yard of tissue lamé fabric, gold

1/4 yard of lighweight woven fusible interfacing

1/4 yard of 100-percent cotton organdy fabric (or thin batting)

YLI Basting & Bobbin thread

Couching fibers and thread

1-1/2 yards of 3/16" rayon cording for ties

1/4" seam allowances

The instructions for the Wine Gift Bag are a slight variation of the Confetti Gift Bag above. This is to have the four points at the top, adding festivity to this project. This version sports a glitzy lamé lining fabric.

1. Following instructions with the fusible interfacing, iron the interfacing onto the back of the lamé fabric. Trace the pattern for the top of the Wine Gift Bag. Use it and the diagram to make a paper pattern the size and shape indicated. Follow instructions for Confetti Piecing on page 15 to make two pieces the same as the pattern. Cut two each of organdy, and lamé fabrics. Stack the layers: lamé (right side down), organdy, then Confetti (right side up) to have two pieces. Pin. Baste and couch according to instructions for Machine Couching, page 110.

2. Following instructions for Bias Binding on page 139, use one of the Confetti fabrics to make bias 1-1/4" wide by 25" long. Sew and slipstitch the bias to the four ends as shown in the diagram according to Applying Bias Edging using the Sew 'n Slipstitch Method on page 140. Allow extra fabric at the points by making a small tuck.

3. Sew the two pieces together in a long seam. Zigzag the seam allowance.

4. Fold the bag in half with right sides together, sew and zigzag the side seams.

← fold

5. Pinch the bottom corners into triangu-

lar shapes, and sew across to make seams 3-1/2" long. See step 3 of the Confetti Gift Bag, page 115. Cut away the excess, leaving a 1/4" seam allowance, and zigzag.

6. Tack the center of the cording to one of the seams. Tie a knot at each end of the cording and fray the ends. Tie the cording around the neck of the bottle in a bow.

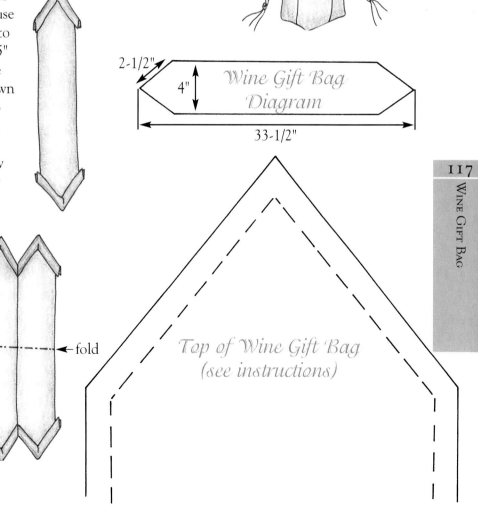

Wine Gift Bag Diagram

2-1/2"

4"

33-1/2"

Top of Wine Gift Bag (see instructions)

$\mathcal{S}$ilk Jewelry Pouch

Size: 3-1/2" wide, by approximately 4-1/2" high.

Silk Jewelry Pouches are little gems themselves.

Materials

Pieces of silk or other lightweight fabrics for crazy patches and casings
4" x 8-1/2" 100-percent cotton muslin for foundation
YLI Basting & Bobbin thread
4" x 8-1/2" silk fabric for lining, any color
100-percent cotton sewing thread to blend with the fabrics
Soie Perlee or other twisted silk threads for embroidery, your choice of colors
1-1/4 yards of 1/8" rayon cording, your choice of color

Note: if making the bag a size other than that shown here, make the casings 2" long x the width of the sewn bag plus 1". See step 3, page 119.

1/4" seam allowances

This silk pouch is designed for a jewelry gift that is extra special. The example shown is made of silk fabrics and threads using the Antique Method of crazy quilting, and is lined in silk. It can be used to store the jewelry when not being worn. Make one to learn the procedure, then you will be able to make additional pouches in other sizes.

1. Use the Antique Method of crazy patching (see page 8) to patch the muslin foundation. Baste around the outer edges of the piece. Work embroidery stitches along patches using the stitches of your choice.

2. With right sides together, machine sew the lining fabric to the patched piece along side seams only. Turn right side out, press.

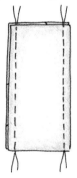

3. Out of any of the silk patch fabrics cut 2 casing pieces each 2" x 4-1/2". Sew one casing piece to each end of the bag as follows: center the piece on the bag with right sides together. Machine sew the seam. Press the casings and seam allowances away from the bag.

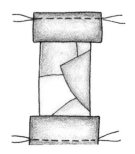

3a. Fold each short end of each casing 1/4" under, then again, press, and pin. Hand stitch to hem the folded edge to the casing.

3b. Fold the long edge of the casing under 1/4", match the folded edge to the seamline, press, and slipstitch by hand.

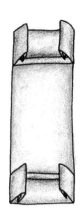

4. Leaving the casings unsewn, slipstitch the sides of the bag stitching through the crazy patched piece in order to conceal the lining. Cut two lengths of cording each 22" long. Using a safety pin, thread one through both of the casings and knot the ends. Thread the second length in the opposite direction, then knot the ends.

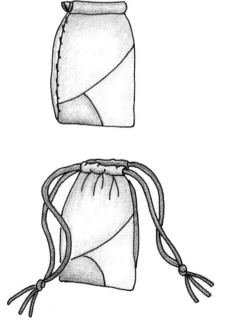

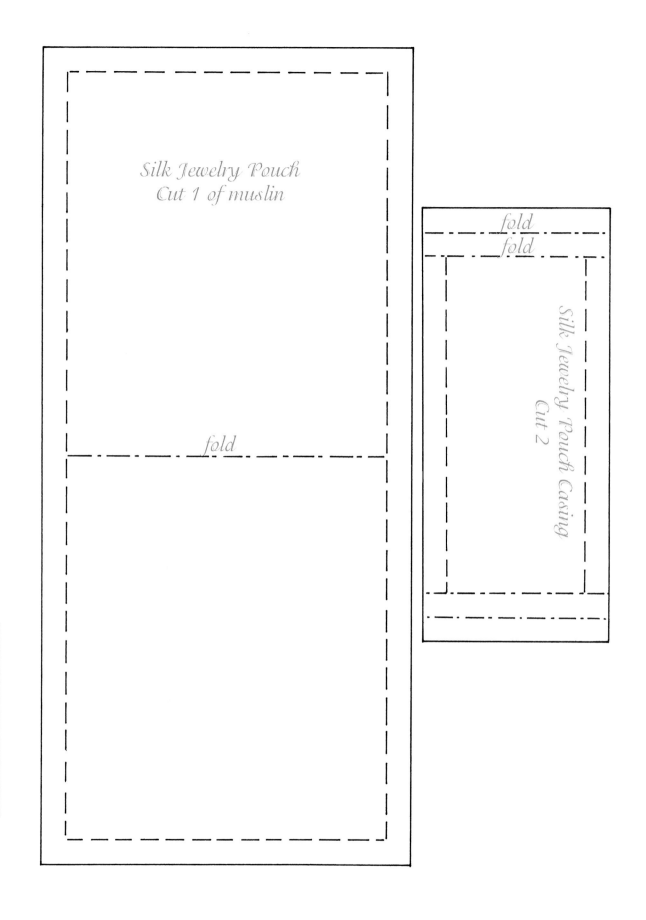

Silk Jewelry Pouch
Cut 1 of muslin

fold

Silk Jewelry Pouch Casing
Cut 2

fold
fold

Silk Doll and Moon Ornaments

Size: approximately 4" x 4-1/2" when folded.

The Moon and Doll Ornaments are tasseled; they're unique decorations to use for any occasion.

Materials

Silk fabric scraps in the colors of your choice
Small piece of 100-percent cotton muslin for each ornament foundation
Pearl Crown Rayon threads in the colors of your choice
100-percent cotton sewing thread to blend with the fabrics
4" rayon tassels, two for each doll, one for the moon
1-1/3 yards of rayon cording for each ornament
12" of gold hanging cord for each ornament
1" (or 25 mm) wood bead with 3/8" hole, one for each doll
1-1/4" x 3-1/4" piece of silver embroidery leather* for Moon ornament
Small amount of stuffing for each ornament
Tracing paper, pencil, scissors

*Embroidery leather is available from Kreinik Mfg. Co. Inc. – see Sources.

1/4" seam allowance.

The fanciful shapes of these ornaments are constructed of silk fabrics using the Antique Method of crazy quilting. They can be adapted for various holiday uses by choosing different colors.

1. Trace and cut out the patterns for the ornaments. Cut two pieces of muslin for each ornament. Cut out one leather face for the moon. Following instructions for the Antique Method on page 8, use the silk scraps to patch each of the muslin pieces. Embroider along patch seams using the stitches and thread colors of your choice.

2. For each ornament: Place the two crazy quilted pieces right sides together and sew between the dots on the patterns. Trim the seams, turn right sides out, and lightly press. Stuff each ornament.

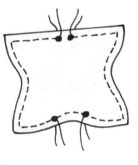

3. To finish the doll ornaments: Sew the larger opening closed. Cut the rayon cording into 4 equal pieces. Hold the pieces to-gether and knot 1" from one end. Place the bead onto the cording, and slide it down to the knot. (If the knot is too small to hold the bead in place, tie a second knot over the first.) Tie a knot at the top of the bead. Glue can be ap-plied to the inside of the bead if needed. Push the short end of the cording into the small open-ing at the top of the doll body, allowing the fabric to turn under slightly. Slipstitch the fabric to the knot of the cording. Ravel the long end of the cording to make kinky hair.

4. To finish the moon: press under the open seam allowances of the opening, in-sert the leather face piece, and stitch the fabric to the leather with small stitches along the seamlines.

5. Knot the hanging cord and stitch to the doll's hair at the knots, and to the top of the moon. Sew on tassels as shown in the photograph.

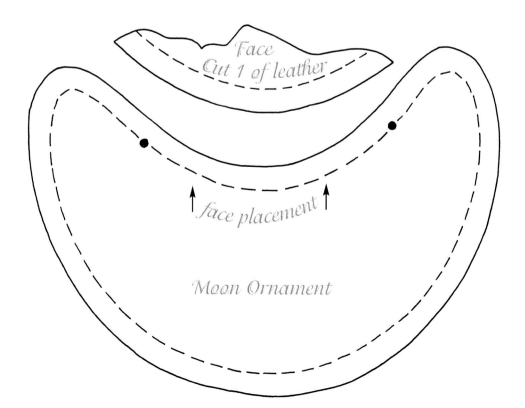

Face
Cut 1 of leather

↑ face placement ↑

Moon Ornament

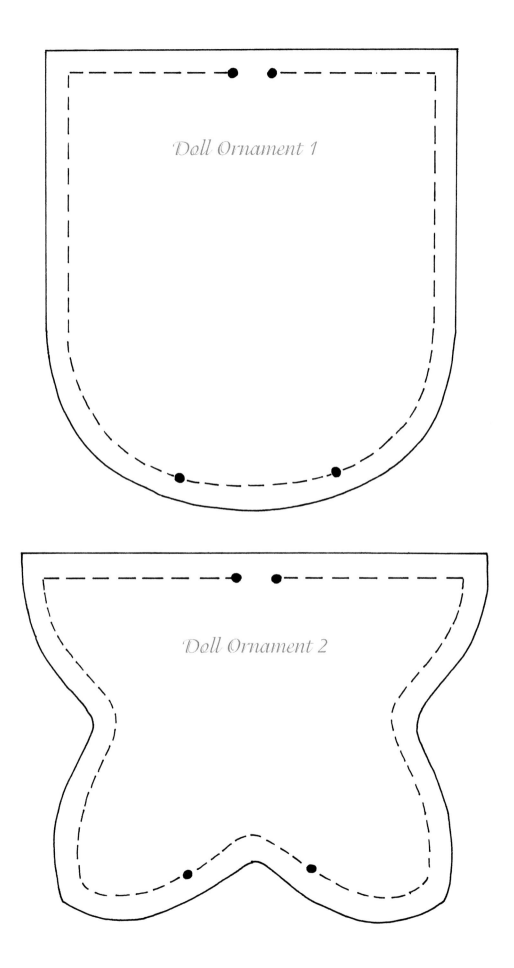

Doll Ornament 1

Doll Ornament 2

Dog's Jacket

Bear-Bear, a sheepdog, doesn't need extra warmth even in the cold of winter, so his jacket was made without batting or interlining. He has been very cooperative in having his jacket fitted and will wear it with the orange side out during deer hunting season because he lives near the woods.

Right. The Dog Jacket is draped over the back of a chair to show its shape.

Materials

(Amounts of fabric and batting will depend on the size of the dog; see instructions.)

Tape measure, chalk or pencil

Scrap fabric for fitting the dog

1/4 yard lengths of 8 different quilting cotton fabrics (see Confetti Piecing, page 15)

100-percent cotton sewing thread to blend with the fabrics

Cotton flannel or plain cotton fabric for backing (use orange if making a reversible hunting-season jacket; consider weight of fabric for amount of warmth needed)

Cotton or poly batting, optional

Cotton fabric ties (see instructions)

If your dog is not adequately furred for cold climates, he or she will be delighted to have a cozy quilted jacket. Follow the directions to make a custom-fitted jacket. To keep a dog cozy, use cotton flannel for the backing fabric and a thick batting. If the dog needs a light cover, use a plain cotton backing fabric and do not include a batting. If you live in a rural area, use a brilliant orange fabric for the backing fabric so your dog can wear it orange-side-out during hunting season.

1. Begin by fitting the dog. If the dog is wiggly, do this by measuring. If the dog will stand still, you can drape the scrap fabric over the dog and cut it to fit. Observe the diagram for the general shape of the jacket, although you can make any variations on that shape that you prefer. The jacket shown here is longer around the dog's shoulders, and shorter at the tail end.

To measure the dog, first determine the length of the jacket measuring from the top of the shoulders to the tail. Then measure to find the depth of the jacket at the dog's shoulder, and then its hips.

2. Transfer the measurements to the scrap fabric (indicate by using pins or chalk). Lay the fabric folded lengthwise onto a flat surface to be sure that both sides are cut the same. Round the corners as shown in the diagram. Place the fabric on the dog to check the fit. Measure to find how long the four ties should be. Allow extra length for tying a bow.

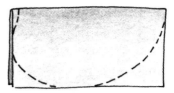

3. Following Confetti Piecing instructions on page 15, make Confetti to fit the size of the fabric pattern, and cut out the shape from the Confetti. Cut the backing fabric and the batting the same. Layer the backing, batting, and the Confetti top as they will be when finished. Pin, baste, and then tie the layers (see page 139). Baste around the outer edges.

4. Measure around the outer edge of the jacket, and make 1-1/4" wide bias binding out of the additional 1/2 yard of fabric, see Bias Binding instructions page 139. Follow instructions for Applying Bias Edging using the Sew 'n Slipstitch Method on page 140 to sew on the binding.

5. Cut four ties, each 3" wide by the determined lengths. For each tie, fold the piece lengthwise with right sides together and sew along the long edge and one short end. Turn right side out. Press. Turn the raw edges inward 1/4", then topstitch completely around each tie. Attach the ties to the jacket with safety pins and place the jacket on the dog to check the placements of the ties. When placed correctly, topstitch the ties to the jacket.

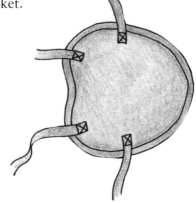

Chapter 8

*B*oudoir and *B*eyond

The three boudoir projects are heirloom pieces.

An Alphabet to Embroider

A frilly boudoir pillow, luxurious silk scarf, and a set of miniature purses are the focus of this chapter. The pillow is a perfect and useful accent for a window seat or on a bed, and is easy to make using the Confetti method of crazy piecing.

A scarf is a versatile accessory and a way to wear a touch of crazy quilting without making a whole garment. Try draping it over the shoulders of a plain, black evening dress or a dark blazer, or wrapped around the waist and held with a pin. Make the scarf any size you like. The one shown here is wide enough to be worn as a stole or around the neck with one end flung to the back. Secure the scarf with a tack or other jewelry pin.

Make and wear a little pendant bag to hold your car keys, a lipstick, or pocket change. It is sure to draw many compliments! This little item will help you practice your patching and embellishing skills in a small format—and what a perfect gift idea.

Projects:

Initial Pillow

Silk Evening Scarf

Pendant Purses

Materials

Photocopier
Tissue paper, pencil
Fabric for embroidery background
Embroidery threads of your choice

The initial embroidery is being worked in a 14" lap hoop, a hoop that is large enough to complete the initial without having to move it to different parts of the design. A lap hoop is supported above a base so that both hands are free to work the embroidery. The Tracing Paper Transfer Method is being used.

Detail of the embroidered initial.

An Alphabet to Embroider

Use a photocopier (or hand-sketch) to enlarge the individual letters to an appropriate size for your project. The "A" used in the Initial Pillow is reproduced to about 5" high. Transfer the enlarged letter by using the Tissue Paper Transfer Method (see page 141).

The "A" shown here was embroidered on 100-percent cotton sateen fabric. The embroidery materials used include size 8 and size 12 pearl cottons, 4 mm silk ribbon, and white seed beads. Mix and match the embroidery materials of your own choice. Use the stitches indicated in the diagram, or use the ones of your own choosing. The Outline Stitch is commonly used for outlining embroidery designs, but you may also use Backstitch, Chain Stitch, or French Knots for outlining. Fill in with a design as I have here, or fill in solidly. Also feel free to substitute embroideries of other types of flowers, placing them around the letter as desired.

This pillow is easy to make using the Confetti method of crazy piecing. Work white-on-white embroidery to embroider the initial of your choice following instructions for An Alphabet to Embroider, on page 129. Choose fabrics that are predominantly white and/or ecru, to go with the embroidery, white laces and batiste.

Old linens can sometimes suggest ideas for embroidery designs.

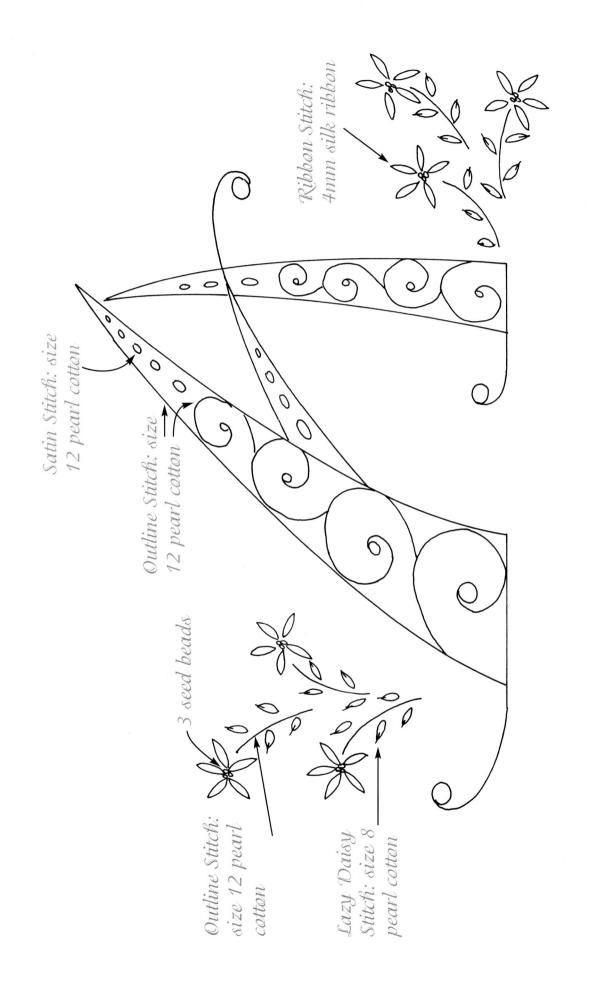

Ribbon Stitch:
4mm silk ribbon

Satin Stitch: size
12 pearl cotton

Outline Stitch: size
12 pearl cotton

3 seed beads

Outline Stitch:
size 12 pearl
cotton

Lazy Daisy
Stitch: size 8
pearl cotton

Initial Pillow

Size: 18" long (not including the tied ends) by approximately 7-3/4" high.

The Initial Pillow is shown with the Ladies and Fans silk crazy quilt.

Materials

Paper, pencil, ruler, scissors
3/4 yard of 100-percent cotton muslin
100-percent cotton sewing thread, white
Stuffing
12" x 14" piece of 100-percent cotton sateen fabric for embroidery, white, and embroidery materials (see An Alphabet to Embroider, page 128)
1/4 yard each of 8 different quilting cotton fabrics including prints with ecru, white, and grey-blue backgrounds (see Confetti Piecing, page 15)
1 yard of 100-percent cotton batiste fabric, white
2-1/2 yards of 3/16" cotton filler cord
1-3/4 yards of 2-1/2" wide eyelet lace, white
1-1/3 yards of 1/4" wide satin ribbon, white

1/4" seam allowances

Make the pillow insert

1. Measure and cut out an 8-1/4" square piece of paper. Fold the paper evenly into quarters, and measure and mark to draw 1/4 of a circle 8-1/4" in diameter. Cut along the marks to make the complete circle.

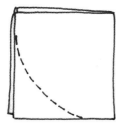

2. Cut the muslin into one piece 18-1/2" x 24-1/2", and two 8-1/4" circles using the paper pattern.

3. Sew the 18-1/2" ends together to form a tube, leaving 6" at the center of the seam unsewn. Press the seam open, but do not turn. Pin a circle to one end of the tube, and sew around. Repeat for the other end.

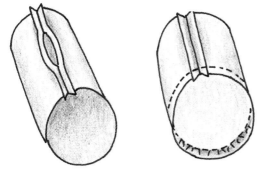

4. Turn the insert right side out and stuff firmly, packing the stuffing carefully to keep the ends flat and avoiding lumps. Hand-sew the opening closed. Set the insert aside.

Make the pillow

1. Cut a piece of muslin the same size as the cotton sateen fabric, place it on the back of the sateen fabric and handle the two as one. Follow the instructions for An Alphabet to Embroider on page 128 to embroider the initial of your choice on the sateen fabric. Make a paper pattern 9-1/2" wide x 8" high, and then cut the 4 corners diagonally. Use the pattern to cut out the initial.

2. Follow instructions for the Confetti method on page 15 to make one piece 22-1/2" x 18-1/2" using one to two cuts of the cotton quilting fabrics.

3. From the batiste fabric, cut two pieces each 11" x 22-1/2". Following instructions for welting on page 142, fold the remaining batiste diagonally and cut bias strips 1-1/2" wide and make 2-1/2 yards of welting using the cotton filler cord. Machine sew the welting around the initial piece, and along the long edges of the Confetti piece.

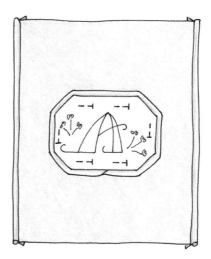

4. Pin the initial onto the center of the Confetti piece, keeping the pins in from the edge.

5. Sew the short ends of the lace together and overcast the seam. Baste along the long raw edge and gather the lace to fit around the initial piece. Pin and arrange the gathers evenly, having the basting line even with the seam of the welting. Hand or machine sew the initial and lace to the Confetti piece, stitching along the seam of the welting.

6. Sew the batiste pieces to the sides of the Confetti piece, sewing along the seams of the welting. Hem the outer edges of the batiste by turning under 1/4", and 1/4" again, and stitch by machine or slipstitch by hand.

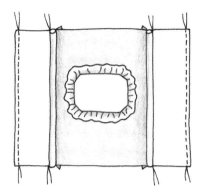

7. With right sides together, sew the bottom seam of the pillow. Push the stuffed insert inside the pillow. Hand-sew a gathering thread in the batiste 4" from the welting seam. Gather and fasten off. Cut the 1/4" satin ribbon into two equal lengths. Hand tack the center of one of the ribbons to the gathers. Tie a bow around the gathers. Repeat for the remaining ribbon.

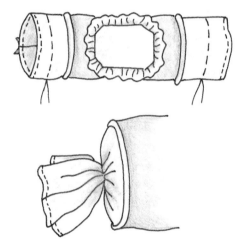

Silk Evening Scarf

Size: Make the scarf the length and width of your choice. The scarf shown here is 15" x 53".

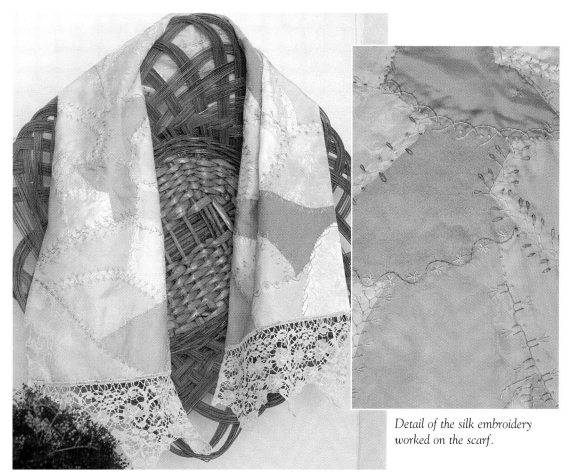

Detail of the silk embroidery worked on the scarf.

A silk scarf is an elegant accessory.

Materials

1 yard of 42" wide silk organza fabric, white

Scraps of silk fabrics: jacquards, habotai, crepe de chine, and others in pastel shades or colors of your choice

YLI Basting & Bobbin thread

8 or more spools of Soie Perlee or other twisted thread for embroidery, assorted light colors

1 yard of lightweight silk backing fabric, any coordinating color

1 yard of wide antique or handmade lace, for the ends of the scarf

1/4" seam allowance

The lace ends on the scarf shown here are salvaged pieces of damaged antique lace. The side edges of the lace are finished by hand sewing on a narrow bias binding made of silk fabric.

For maximum drape, be sure to choose lightweight silk fabrics for this project. Choose the color scheme of your preference; I have used pastels.

1. See "Using Silks" below. Prewash all fabrics, unless your scarf will be dry-cleaned only.

2. Cut and sew the organza fabric into one piece, 15" x 53".

3. Following instructions for the Antique Method on page 8, patch the organza fabric.

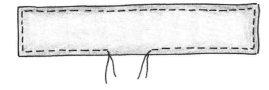

4. Embroider along patch seams with Soie Perlee threads and working two or more rows of embroidery along each.

5. Sew the backing right sides together with the crazy quilted top, leaving an opening to turn. Trim seams if necessary, turn, and press. Hand stitch the opening.

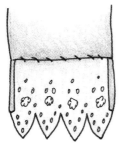

6. Finish the sides of the lace by hand stitching on a narrow bias binding: make Double-fold Bias Tape (cut the bias about 1" wide), following instructions on page 140. Hand sew both edges of the tape to the lace, clean finishing the ends. Hand sew the lace to the ends of the scarf.

A piece of antique lace has its ends finished and is hand sewn to the end of the scarf.

Using Silks

(Also see "Dyeing Silks" on page 103.)

Most silk fabrics are washable. Follow the washing technique given on page 7. Silks are inherently "electric," and if they tend to glue themselves to your hands try adding some humidity to your room. Spritzing the air with water occasionally can help.

Silk organza is a loosely woven fabric with some stiffness to it, making it excellent for foundations. However, it can sometimes skew easily. True up the edges along a desk edge or on a cutting mat as you patch and baste. After the piece is basted it will hold its shape.

As soon as you begin handling silk fabrics and threads, you may feel the need to run to the manicurist to have all of your rough spots smoothed. Silk has a tendency to snag on these areas. To prepare for working with silks, treat your hands to a non-greasy hand lotion, then buff your hands on a clean, dry towel. Keep an emory board handy and smooth any rough spots that become apparent as you work.

Pendant Purses

Colors are not indicated below; mix and match as you like. Choose your fanciest fabric scraps, threads and other materials.

Pendant purses make elegant little accessories and make good use of small bits of the finest materials.

Materials

Tracing paper, pencil, scissors
10" x 5" piece of 100-percent cotton muslin for foundation
10" x 5" piece of taffeta or silk fabric for lining
Fabric scraps, silks and other choice pieces from your collection
Laces, gimpes, braids or sew-on trims of your choice
YLI Basting & Bobbin thread
Pearl Crown Rayon or other embroidery threads, several colors
100-percent cotton sewing thread to blend with the fabrics
Piece of satin or taffeta fabric to make a 12" length of 1-1/4" wide bias binding
A fancy button
1 yard of rayon cording

1/4" seam allowances

Colors are not indicated below; mix and match as you like. Choose your fanciest fabric scraps, threads, and other materials.

1. Trace and cut out the pendant purse pattern. Use the pattern to cut one each of muslin and lining fabrics.

2. Patch the muslin foundation following instructions for the Antique Method on page 8 adding laces or trimmings of your choice along some of the seams. I used five patches per purse.

3. Embroider along patch seams using the embroidery stitches of your choice. Add silk ribbon embroidery or any other embellishments of your choice.

4. Place the lining on the wrong side of the crazy patched piece and baste around. With right sides together fold the purse along the lower fold line. Sew, then zigzag the side seams. Press lightly. Pinch one of the bottom corners to form a triangular shape, centering the side seam. Measure to find where a seam sewn across will be 3/4" long, and sew across the triangle at that point. Repeat for the other bottom corner.

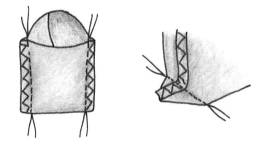

5. Cut a bias strip 1-1/4" wide by 12" long; see Bias Binding instructions, page

139. Follow instructions for Applying Bias Edging using the Sew 'n Slip-stitch Method on page 140 to sew the bias continuously around the upper edge of the purse.

6. Fold the flap down and determine button placement, about 3/8" down from the flap. Sew on the button. Make a thread loop.

7. Make a knot about 2" in from each end of the cording, and sew cording to sides of bag. Fluff the cording ends and trim evenly.

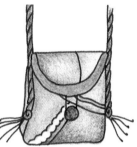

This pendant purse is decorated with a lacy motif.

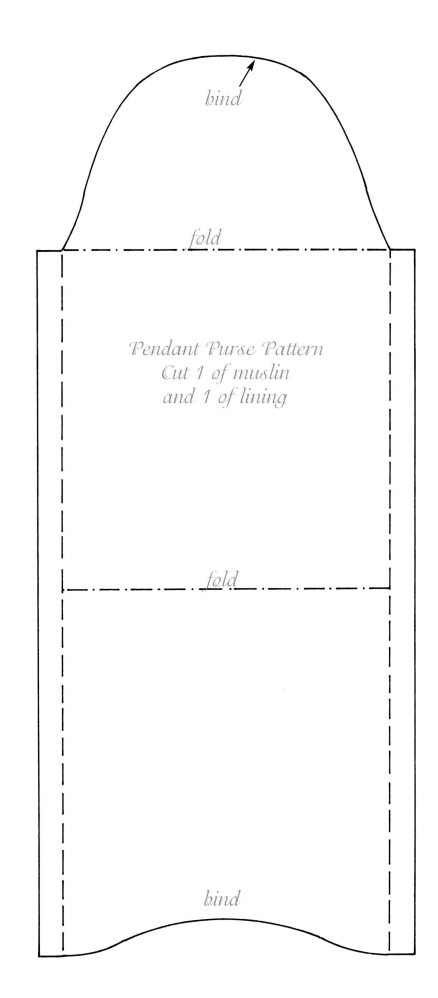

bind

fold

Pendant Purse Pattern
Cut 1 of muslin
and 1 of lining

fold

bind

Basic Techniques

Basting, Pinning

Hand basting is making a line of hand-stitched running stitches to secure layered fabrics. It is used to hold patches in place for the Antique Method of crazy patching, and other purposes. Use YLI Basting & Bobbin thread, or 100-percent cotton sewing thread. If you are using sewing thread, run the thread over beeswax for easier handling. Use any fine hand sewing needle such as a size 12 sharp. Make the stitches about 1/2" to 1" in length.

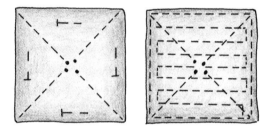

To baste for machine quilting, stack all layers evenly, then pin to secure. Begin basting at the center of the piece, working diagonally to an outer corner. Repeat, working the basting to all outer corners. Then baste back and forth throughout the entire piece in lines about 1" to 1-1/2" apart. Finish by basting around the outer edges.

Pins can be used if the quilt is to be tied, or if machine quilting is minimal. Use safety pins especially made for quilting, and place them to adequately hold the layers in place.

Basting is also a long machine stitch used to hold pieces together before a final line of stitches is sewn that will securely attach all pieces.

Bias Binding

Although bias tape can be purchased and used in place of handmade bindings, the advantage of making your own is that you can choose the fabric, and even use one of the fabrics already used in the project. Begin with a 1/4 to 1/2 yard length of fabric.

a. To cut the bias for binding, first fold the fabric in half diagonally. Press along the fold, then cut along the crease.

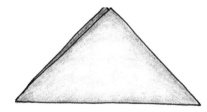

b. Using a rotary cutter, acrylic ruler, and cutting mat, cut strips the width desired.

c. Machine sew the strips together to make the length needed.

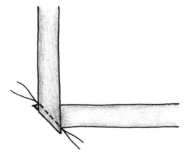

Single-fold Bias Tape

Following instruction for Bias Binding above, cut the bias to the width required. Use a bias-tape maker, or by hand fold the side edges of the bias under approximately 1/4" and press.

Double-fold Bias Tape

Make single-fold bias tape, then fold and press a crease along the center of the tape. To sew on the double-fold tape, place it onto the edge of the piece to be bound, and machine stitch along the bias, through all layers.

Applying Bias Edging using the Sew 'n Slipstitch Method

This method makes a nicer finish than machine-topstitching pre-folded, bias tape.

a. Cut bias strips 1-1/4" wide (for a narrower edging, cut the strips 1-1/8" wide), and sew strips together for the length needed. Machine sew the bias strip with right sides together to the right side of the project (unless instructions specify otherwise) using a 1/4" seam allowance.

b. Fold the bias to the back and press along the seam just sewn.

c. Fold the long raw edge under, press, and, by hand, slipstitch the fold to the project, concealing the seam sewn in (a).

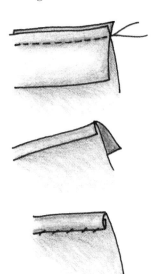

When sewing bias binding completely around the outer edge of a project, begin with a length of bias longer than needed. Fold the short end 1/4" under. Place the bias right sides together with the project, and begin sewing using a 1/4" seam allowance. Sew completely around and finish by overlapping onto the turned-under end and stitching for about 1/2" over the previous stitching. Cut the bias off where the stitching ends.

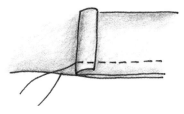

Machine Quilting and Stitching in the Ditch

Quilting joins layered fabrics by means of sewing through all of the layers in a regular or irregular stitching pattern.

Begin by having the layers basted (page 139). To machine quilt, a quilting needle may be used in the machine. Thread the top part of the machine with quilting thread that is suitable for sewing machines, such as YLI's Quilting Thread. Wind the bobbin with 100-percent cotton sewing thread, or YLI Select Thread. Experiment on similar layers of scrap fabric to see whether the tension needs adjustment. Set the machine for a long stitch length, such as 4 mm. Set the tension so the top thread does not come through to the back, and the bobbin thread does not come through to the front.

To begin a line of stitching, leave about 6" of each of the bobbin and top threads hanging. End, leaving about the same.

To fasten off the ends, pull up on the bobbin thread until the top thread peeks through. Using a pin or needle, pull up on the loop thus created, and bring the top thread to the back.

Tie both ends in a square knot at the surface of the fabric. Thread the ends into a hand sewing needle, pierce the backing fabric at the base of the knot, and run the needle between the quilted layers for an inch or a little more, bring the needle up and trim the ends close the surface of the fabric. The ends will disappear inside the layers.

Begin anywhere on the basted piece, and machine-stitch in the pattern of your choice. See individual projects for stitching-pattern suggestions.

Stitching in the Ditch can be done instead of quilting or tying. Simply machine stitch through all layers along the seam lines of the piecing. Match the thread color to the fabrics as much as possible, and try to stitch directly on top of previous stitching. Work as many areas as needed to sufficiently hold the layers in place. Finish thread ends the same as above.

Rod Pocket

This is a "sleeve" of fabric attached to the upper edge of a quilt so that it can be hung on a wall. Cut a length of fabric to the same width as the quilt, and 6" to 8" wide. On each end of the strip, fold the fabric to the back 1/4", then another 1/4", and stitch in place. Fold under and press the long edges 1/4". Place the strip at the upper edge of the back of the quilt and pin. By hand, slipstitch in place.

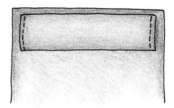

To hang the quilt, slide a dowel through the rod pocket. A decorative curtain rod may also be used.

Slipstitching

This stitch is a hand technique used to sew a folded edge onto another piece, such as in hand-appliqué or applying bias binding. Use 100-percent cotton sewing thread and a fine needle such as a size 12 sharp. Thread the needle and fasten on with a knot or with several tiny stitches made close together. Slide the needle through the folded edge, then pick up a few threads of the other piece, and bring the needle through. Continue, keeping the stitches small and concealed so they barely show, if at all.

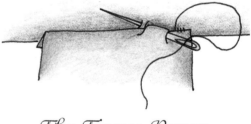

The Tissue Paper Transfer Method

This method appears in my two previous books, and is repeated here because it is the easiest method I have found of transferring a design to be worked in embroidery. It leaves no marks behind on the fabric. You will need ordinary tissue paper (the kind used for gift wrapping), pencil, sewing thread, and a needle.

Cut a piece of tissue paper about 2" larger than the design on all sides. Trace the design onto the tissue paper. Hand baste the tissue to the fabric having the basting stitches just outside the lines of the design. Embroider the outlines of the design, remove the basting stitches, and tear the tissue away from the embroidery stitches. If the outlines will be filled in, the tissue paper is first removed.

Trim Seam and Clip Curves

Trimming the seam removes some of the excess seam allowance, making a neater appearance on the right side. While trimming, a seam allowance that consists of several layers can also be graded, by trimming each of the layers a slightly different width. Be careful to leave enough fabric so the seam retains its strength.

Clipping the seam is done on curves to help the fabric lie smoothly. Clip almost but not quite to the seam at sufficient intervals so that the piece will lie flat.

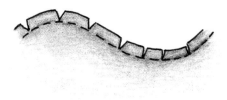

Tying

Tying the layers of a quilted piece is an easy way to hold the layers in place. I most often use size 8 pearl cotton for this.

First, baste the layers of the piece to be tied. Safety pins can be used instead of basting if they hold the layers adequately.

Take a small stitch through all the layers and tie the thread into a square knot.

Make the ties about 4" to 6" apart. On a crazy quilt made of the Antique Method, the thread is often tied on the back of the quilt. On other Confetti pieced projects, the ties can be made on the front.

Welting

Cut bias strips (Bias Binding, page 139) in a width that when folded over the cotton filler cord will leave a seam allowance of at least 1/4". Using 3/16" cotton filler cord, cut the bias 1-1/4" to 1-1/2" wide.

a. Machine sew bias strips together to obtain the length needed. With a zipper foot on the sewing machine, fold the bias over the cording and stitch along the cord. A long basting stitch may be used for this. Trim the seam allowance of the welting so it is even. If the project has 1/4" seam allowances, try to have a 1/4" welting seam allowance.

b. Stitch again along the seam of the welting when attaching the welting to the project, this time using a regular stitch length.

c. Press the seam to the back.

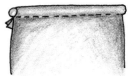

If the welting is sewn completely around a project, end the stitching at the same point where it first began. Then, push back the fabric from the cord (or pull on the cord while pushing back the fabric) at each end, and trim off the cord so it will not overlap. Fold the excess fabric to the back and Stitch in the Ditch (see page 140) to secure.

Sources

Many items shown in this book are commonly available. Look for waste canvas in needle-point shops, fancy fabrics in stores that sell garment and drapery fabrics, 100-percent cotton fabrics in quilting shops, and so on. Other items can be found at the sources listed below.

Books of cross-stitch charts, and iron-on transfers for shadow work, silk ribbon, and other embroidery
Dover Publications, Inc.
31 East 2nd Street
Mineola, NY 11501

Hook and loop fastener, tassels, cotton filler cording, laces, rayon cording, trims
Home Sew
P.O. Box 4099
Bethlehem, PA 18018-0099
Web site: www.homesew.com

Metallic cord, braids, and ribbons, Silk Serica® (silk thread) and embroidery leather.
Kreinik Mfg. Co., Inc.
3106 Timanus Lane, Suite 101
Baltimore, MD 21244
800-537-2166
Web site: www.kreinik.com

Silk fabrics
Thai Silks
252 State St.
Los Altos, CA 94022
Web site: www.thaisilks.com

Silk and other fabrics for dyeing, dyes
Rupert, Gibbon & Spider
P.O. Box 425
Healdsburg, CA 95448

Battenberg lacemaking supplies
Lacis
3163 Adeline St.
Berkeley, CA 94703
Web site: www.lacis.com

Instant-setting silk dyes, kits, supplies
Things Japanese
9805 N.E. 116th St., Suite 7160
Kirkland, WA 98034-2287

Silk ribbons, Basting & Bobbin Thread, YLI Pearl Crown Rayon Thread®, YLI Quilting Thread™; YLI Select Thread™, 1000 Denier Silk Embroidery Thread
YLI Corporation
161 West Main St.
Rock Hill, SC 29730
800-296-8139
Web site: www.ylicorp.com

Also by the Author

Ribbon Embroidery, Dover Publications, 1997
Instructions and stitches for silk ribbon embroidery, iron-on transfers.

The Magic of Crazy Quilting, Krause Publications, 1998
Complete instructions, four methods, embellishment techniques, 100 embroidery stitches, 1,000 stitch variations.

Shadow Work Embroidery, Dover Publications, 1999
Instructions, iron-on transfers. Transfers can be used for other types of embroidery as well.

Crazy Quilts by Machine, Krause Publications, 2000
Designs for quilts, table toppers, pillows, throws, and complete instructions for both machine and hand work. Includes an 'encyclopedia' of machine techniques for embroidery and embellishments.

Detail from the Browns & Golds Strippie Quilt (Crazy Quilts by Machine).

Index

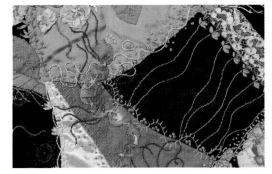

Detail from the Piano Shawl (The Magic of Crazy Quilting).

Detail from the Victorian Elegance quilt (Crazy Quilts by Machine).